When Everyone Shines but You

When Everyone Shines but You

Saying Goodbye to 'I'm Not Good Enough'

Kelly Martin

First Printing: 2014
ISBN-13: 978-1499698886
Being Human Publishing
Gloucester, Gloucestershire,
United Kingdom.

www.kellymartin.co.uk

Ordering Information:

Special discounts are available on quantity purchases by corporations, associations, educators and others. For details, contact the publisher at the above listed address.

U.S. trade bookstores and wholesalers please contact:

Being Human Publishing, email <kellymartin@kellymartin.co.uk>

Cover Design: Kelly Martin

Cover Image: George Hodan

Editing: Michael Doherty

Disclaimer:

This information in this book is not intended as a substitute for consultation with healthcare or other professionals. Any use of the information herein is at the reader's sole discretion and risk. Neither the author nor the publisher can be held responsible for any loss, claim, or damage arising out of the use or misuse of any, or all, of the information contained herein.

To my best friend Michael as a testament to his empowering presence in this world and to everyone who has ever felt like a failure in life.

It's time now for all the square pegs, black sheep and 'not enough' stories to be laid to rest.

~Contents~

~Acknowledgements~

As this book was written behind closed doors as a secret and sacred experience there is one person who without his emotional support, his diligent and focused editing needs a huge amount of gratitude and that person is my best friend Michael Doherty. Michael's consistent encouragement when the 'Failure Story' was playing inside my head kept nudging me forward. So thanks from the bottom of my heart Michael, your help, love and friendship has empowered my journey.

And lastly a big thank you to those button pushers out there that triggered painful experiences within me, without which this book would never have been written.

Thank you!

~Foreword~

This book that you're holding in your hand, or reading on a screen, goes against the general run of self-help books, which tell you that you're less than perfect, that you need to be different from the way you are, that you're broken and need fixing.

The message of this book is that you're not broken – you don't need fixing; that being human, with all its seemingly negative aspects is OK. Not just OK, but perfect.

Kelly Martin gives you permission to be who you are, just as you are, warts and all. She explains that it's just not possible to be all positive, that we live in a world of contrast, of opposites, where positive and negative are the two ends of the same stick; that without the negative there can be no positive either.

Kelly explains in simple, easy to understand terms that trying to suppress negative emotions only makes them more powerful, only feeds them with more energy, and that they will always force their way through to the surface, even stronger than before, often at the most inappropriate times; that it's like tying down the lid of a pressure cooker. It will explode, and you'll wish it hadn't.

Kelly shows us that not only is it damaging to try to suppress our negative thoughts, emotions and feelings, but that they are a gift, jewels, and that by embracing them, by accepting them as a natural part of who we are, by giving them our caring attention, they will help us access our true nature, who we really are, stripped of control, manipulation, and all the usual traits and behaviours of our egos.

Kelly explains how all our efforts and strivings can be counterproductive, that we can achieve more by going with the natural flow of life, by allowing rather than forcing.

You may find that these are radical ideas, which go against the grain of everything we've been taught in western society, against much of our social conditioning, goal setting, and emphasis on the positive.

I recommend that you approach this powerful book with an open mind, and that you take it slowly.

Above all, enjoy.

Michael Doherty
Gloucester UK 2014
(Author of 'I Ching - A Beginner's Guide')

~Preface~

There comes a time in life when the answers to pressing questions cannot be found outside of us and this book was written in response to an inner dialogue seeking resolution.

After 30+ years of painful anxiety, feelings of intense failure and low self-worth, I grew frustrated by the books out there that didn't answer my questions. After years of diligently following teachers of the Law of Attraction and the positive thinking culture, I felt something was missing. Something didn't add up. So much of what I read was focused on 'creating reality'; on changing thoughts from 'negative' to 'positive', but it simply felt very out of balance.

With the best will in the world none of the methods I saw worked for me and I thought to myself one day, *'I can't be the only one feeling this way'*.

I was looking for a book not yet written. An inner response to the questions many people had, including me. This book is the result.

This book was written often in the midst of some inner challenge. It felt almost as if life was offering me the opportunity to gain some answers from the darkness I was experiencing. I now realise that none of this book would have been written had I not been feeling challenged. I was to go caving, caving for the jewels within the pain, the suffering and the difficulties.

During intense rage; during sadness; during jealousy and frustration; words came through me, from a place I did not know existed within. I thought other people had access to this wisdom, not me.

So this book was written in a deeply human and also deeply heart-centered way. I allowed my spirit to merge with the human me wanting answers, and my whole self worked as one.

It was a challenge to allow the answers to come some days, because I was bringing to light topics like rage and jealousy that are sometimes frowned upon in spiritual circles. But I felt such a strong desire to make peace with my human self and this is how this book came about.

'When Everyone Shines But You' was almost not written because the story playing inside had me believe I needed to be perfect and fully healed before publishing a book, but something called me forward.

It was a cry from my humanity, a cry for it to be accepted fully as it is right now, to allow myself to be fully human and from there the journey began.

~Introduction~

You are about to go on a journey, on a journey of deep acceptance, a very human journey where your personality and spirit meet as one.

It is time to embrace all of who you are including those human parts of you that may feel disdainful - your flaws, your inner wars.

In many ways this book was not written by me, but was written through me. It is a book where the human personality craves knowledge, compassion and understanding. It is a journey where the hurt, frightened human-self simply wants to know that it matters, that it's here for a reason and it needs reminding of the value of its experience.

Working together as one, the spirit and the human, no separation, both are fuelling the instincts in the other for both questions and answers.

This book addresses many of the aspects of being human that are often hidden on the spiritual path, the life journey. Those personality quirks and challenges like rage, anger, jealousy, frustration and sadness are brought into the loving warm heart of understanding. On this journey you will begin to see that all of your life has a purpose, that no human emotion is to be berated or dismissed, that even those most difficult feelings carry within them the answers and opportunities for self-acceptance, love and compassion.

The journey through your humanity, unveiling your own personal gifts and talents, allowing yourself to be seen, to be accepted and the knowing that who you are matters, that who you are, right now (not when you are perfect or fixed) is of real value.

'**When Everyone Shines But You**' will reveal to you a process of life without force, a more effortless awakening to who you really are, a more mindful approach to living and a surrender to the grace of this journey.

There will be no exercises to practice, or steps to complete. This is the journey. Your human self needs to know that life knows the way and through understanding and a willingness to embrace all of you, your life will begin to flow in ways you may have never thought possible.

Enjoy this journey through your human self, which carries within it all the answers you ever wanted to know and much, much more.

Blessings and love
Kelly x

Chapter 1

~Surrender & Letting Go~

The outer world, society, has led you to believe that for your life to work you need to take control. It has led you to believe that you need to 'will it' into the shape or form you desire. This is simply not true.

There is nothing you need to do perfectly in this world. Yet your desire to get things right, to be right, can prevent you from moving forward at all. As you live your human life there may be a desire to control your life circumstances, to take the reins and exert force or will on an unwanted life experience. This is not only counter-productive, but can make you miss what is naturally unfolding in your life.

You mold your world as you allow it to unravel and unfold, moment by moment, day by day.

This is not a lazy way; this is not a 'sitting on your ass doing nothing' way; this is the natural way that life brings you exactly what you need as and when you need it.

The trees in the autumn do not scream to let their leaves go; they simply change into trees without leaves, and as summer arrives they are then trees with leaves and buds. No attachment to outcome, no attachment to anything. They simply 'are' - in that space between thoughts, between words, that space that is always transforming, always changing – never the same.

The human need for perfection is the mind's need to control what it sees and experiences. The mind needs to grab onto something to feel of value, yet the real value of living comes in the flow of the river, the clouds floating across the sky, the baby being born, the human dying, the air you breathe. All of nature mirrors true perfection. Not 'willing' or 'controlling' perfection. There is no desire in nature to be perfect. It simply is, by embracing the one constant in life – change.

As humans you often find it difficult to trust, to have faith in what seems to be an invisible unknown, an uncertain future. Yet life gave you the greatest teacher – the nature surrounding you which can teach you far more than your scholars or books will ever do. Nature is the effortless teacher, which humanity needs more than ever to hear and listen to now.

In the midst of your stress, or when thoughts are causing you to struggle within, you may feel a rushing, desperate feeling inside you, the desire to do something, anything, to make this feeling change.

You may look outside and see your life falling apart, a loved one may leave you, your finances may collapse, your friendships may disappear; you may feel all alone. Your first response is to take action to try to fix whatever it is that needs to change for things to be alright with you and your world. This rarely works. For in the exerting of your will and the trying to fix the very problem you perceive, it merely grows stronger and bigger. You fight against what you already know to be true, but your human mind wants to stop it from being true.

The gift you can give yourself is to stop in that moment; stop what you are doing right now. Where are you in this moment? Fearing the future? Trying to control what is? But **'What is'** – is! You cannot control your outer world any more than a tree can stop a bolt of lightning striking it down to its core. You cannot stop babies being born if it's their time to be born, nor can you stop people from dying if it's their time to leave planet Earth. They are all part of this transforming universe, all part of this changing flow called life.

For many of you there is this illusion that you can change the outer world, that if you just do x, y or z, the outcome will be different. But different from what?

If change is coming, change comes. If things are to remain the same, they remain the same, for now. No amount of effort or control can make any difference here.

The greatest gift you can give yourself is surrender - surrender to 'what is'.

Some great teachers are coming forward now, to bring this message to you, and yet so many people are still struggling against this. I understand.

You are conditioned to believe that if you let go, if you surrender, you will either be a victim of circumstances and not assertive in your own being, or you will be viewed as being lazy, lacking in willpower, and un-motivated.

Yet will and power cannot exist alongside one another. Motivation does not come into question when you surrender fully into the present moment. Motivation to do, to take action, to make moves, comes naturally from this surrender.

Surrender does not mean sitting on a meditation cushion all day trying to be a higher being. It comes from your evolving nature of being - your nature. You are nature. The trees, the grass, the flowers, the sky, and the grand mountains, they are not here by chance. They are not here to simply act as beautiful art in your life's landscape. No, they are your biggest wakeup call if you can only just look, listen and take them all in.

It's not always easy as a human to walk a different path in life. Especially when the world surrounds you with doers, motivators, assertive individuals, all full of action and desire, wanting to tell you to get off your ass and do something amazing!

But what if you are amazing as you are, right now, reading this, listening to music, observing that tree or cloud over there, wondering if there is more to life than this endless desire for human perfection?

And to step away from the crowd, to be a sheep no more, to walk your own path, to not look to see who is in front of you or who is behind you, to make decisions moment by moment on what is right for you - this is perfection - this is true perfection.

Learn to dance in this space. If you look ahead to where all others are striding forward, wanting to stampede through the next door, the next change, the next new thing, and then you look back and more are coming, more are wanting to get from 'a to b', you see the desire they want to manifest, and once they reach that door they see the next door.

But why not be one of those people, who instead of looking for the next door, lives in the moment, dances in that empty space, that space of now, that space that is not really empty, but full of possibility, full of life, full of living, full of divine perfection?

You know within you, that nature is your nature, that you have all you need in this moment. It blossoms, you blossom. It changes, you change. Nothing is set in stone and no amount of efforting will cause your world to change.

You live in a competitive culture. Society encourages you to be better than everybody else. Instead of hunting and eating your competitors as the animal kingdom does, you taunt, tease and berate one another.

You claim that your efforts to do well and to be a success in the world are for your own wellbeing, but behind many of you there is this desire to prove yourself to others, to prove those people wrong who may have dismissed you, to feel better by comparing with someone who seems worse off than you, and to belittle and begrudge those who have what you really want. But it's not what you really want that you're experiencing in them, it's what you think you want and it's what you think they have, but you have no way of knowing that they have it.

What you really want is to know that you matter.

Chapter 2

~Not Good Enough~

Forgetting Your True Nature

There are many fears in the world. Fear of spiders, enclosed spaces, heights etc., but a major fear I see on planet Earth is the fear of 'not being good enough'. Feeling that as you are is not good enough, so you strive to be better, to be more, to be better than your fellow man, when in fact you are vast and far more expansive than any of you can imagine.

Because of 'not enough'-itis, many of you feel that life is unfair. You feel that you work hard and get nowhere. You see others doing very little, working far less and perhaps not doing a great job, and yet they receive praise and admiration and seem to be valued far more than you are. This hurts you to your core, but your inner being knows that you are far more than this shell, far more than the value you place on outer results and actions. However, human feedback is something you've been taught to need and if you don't receive positive acknowledgment, you doubt your own worth.

The value you place on what you do is important, for the world is your mirror, and if you feel you are not valued, if you feel that your abilities are not seen or heard, you do not feel that you matter.

The outer world is like your mother. It may appear that your mother is conditional in her love, where she loves others for doing exactly what you do, but does not love you. In fact she is reflecting your own mistrust in your own abilities. The world does not see you, or hear you, or know that you exist until you know you exist.

If you feel that who you are isn't important, that what you do doesn't matter, then no amount of effort is going to make a difference to how the world sees you. If you follow your passion, love what you do and value yourself, the world will reflect this.

Someone could paint a black dot on a white piece of paper and receive praise, love, positive feedback and money from that work of art – simply because they feel that what they do is worthwhile. They feel that what they do has meaning and purpose.

The next person could paint another abstract work of art, full of depth, full of colour and fabulous to the eyes, yet no-one will get to see it. To the world, it doesn't exist; it is meaningless. It means nothing because the painter has listened to the stories of his or her past, and believes them.

The painter believes that he or she is worthless, useless, bad at art. And so the world reflects this belief. Both works of art could be held in a prominent visible place where thousands of people pass every single day and yet the black dot on the white paper will receive the most attention.

It's not what you do in this world, but how you feel about what you do that's important.

When you look at your passions, your interests, and your own self, and see nothing of worth, then know that life will feed this belief back to you. If you can find a way to value yourself without exerting your will or your effort anymore, you will find that you need to do less, to shine more.

Shine more!

There is something within you that is wanting to emerge and greet this magnificent world.

Your invisibility serves no-one.

You deserve to be seen.

You deserve to be heard.

You deserve to let your magic out and for life to be a glorious adventure.

Do you think you're ready? It is time to remove the mask of invisibility; it is time to embrace the wonder of you.

No longer may you hide behind that rock, sobbing that no-one can see you - you can come out from behind the rock and allow yourself to be seen now.

Are you ready?

Are you ready for the world to see you and embrace you?

Chapter 3

~It's All So Unfair~

Unfair - the world is unfair, life is unfair, people doing better than you is unfair, people richer, more beautiful, happier than you, all these bring up intense feelings of the word 'unfair'.

Life can feel a cruel and unfair place to be. It can feel a struggle to get past, to go beyond the anger, the rage, the resentment, the feeling of inequality in the world – to go beyond 'unfair'.

So what is really going on here? Why do so many of you feel life is unfair? What is beneath this feeling of unyielding unfairness?

Many of you have been battered and bruised by life's experiences, be it emotionally, mentally, or physically (sometimes all of these). To the human mind, to the ego, this can seem unjust and deeply unfair.

Going beyond Feeling Life Is Unfair

How do you, as a human, go beyond this feeling that 'life is unfair?' The first thing you must do is to let yourself feel this deep unjust feeling taking place.

So many of you think you do allow this feeling, but you don't. You thrash around with the feeling of 'life is unfair', but alongside that goes guilt, a feeling that there is something wrong with you for feeling so angry, so raging, so resentful of other people. And so you are tied together with not only this feeling of unfairness, but all the other emotions that prevent you from acknowledging your own suffering, your own pain.

You beat yourself up for your hate, your anger and your rage, because society frowns upon these feelings and emotions. Your religious and your spiritual teachers encourage compassion, encourage kindness, and encourage viewing the bigger picture. They incite you to feel something you may be unable to feel at that time, and in so doing, you build up this resistance to the very thing that could bring you incredible relief – allowing.

You beat and beat and beat at yourself inside, calling yourself names, making you wrong. So many of you, because of your life experiences, have so little good to say about yourselves, that you try to fight against some honest feelings taking place within you, which simply exacerbates the feelings you were not wanting to feel in the first place.

Am I saying: *"Go out into the world and rage at the world"*? No.

Am I saying: *"Go out to another human and scream at them that it's unfair that they're doing so well and you're not"*? No, because none of this is about anyone else. It's all about you.

If one person who causes you to feel resentment vanishes from your life, another exact copy (often with even greater success and confidence) will appear.

You may have heard before, that those who challenge you the most are here to teach you, and you may have dismissed this and sworn at whoever was sharing this idea, but it's true. No human, no life experience appears in your world without a gift. Those who bring up the most powerful reactions are your greatest teachers, and they may teach you in ways you would rather they did not.

For some of you, your greatest wisdom, your greatest inspiration, your greatest success, comes from feeling that you are at the bottom of the pile of life, or what you may see as the black hole of living. To embrace the gift that you are, the gift that you came to bring into this world, you may have to experience a feeling of unworthiness, a lack of success in the material sense, a lack of confidence, a feeling that you indeed have no purpose, for you to realise that your purpose is greater than you can possibly see right now. And the rage, the resentment, the anger, the *'life is unfair'*, the *'those people are rubbing my nose in it'* type of feelings, are your road through to remembering your essence, to remembering who you really are.

Thank them, for they are a gift. Perhaps not in the midst of the rage, but find a moment of quiet in your day to thank them inwardly for 'pushing your buttons', for they are allowing you to go beyond your limited perception of who you are.

Feeling your feelings can seem to be the most impossible task at times. When faced with intense rage, you may see someone doing exactly what you want to be doing in life, and perhaps it appears that they came about it somewhat effortlessly, perhaps they are much younger than you and seem to be flying through life. The thoughts that arise from within your suffering may sound something like this:

"Look at her! Who does she think she is?"
"Who does he think he is? The sun shines out of his ass!"
"They just like to rub their success in my face"

And from these thoughts, you may go into a tirade of abuse and blame directed at these people, and from that experience you go into self-abuse, beating yourself up mentally and emotionally. Then you feel bad for feeling those feelings, but not just for feeling that they are bad feelings, but also for feeling that you are bad.

Being gentle with yourself can feel extremely challenging during a rage feeling. But at some point the rage will still be there, but it will seem softer. It is in this moment you can stop and feel the feeling. And this does not mean you question the feeling. This is the old western psychology route. No, you simply say what you are feeling, inside, or verbally.

You can now be a watcher of this feeling, even labelling it gently, 'rage, rage'. This may help you to objectify the feeling. You will realise that you are not the rage; you are more than the rage.

Most of all do not ask: *'Where did this come from? How can I change this? What can I do to fix this or get rid of it?'* This is a natural thing to do. You are taught that you need to fix a problem, yet this is not a problem.

It is a moment in time, a moment in life, a moment where you simply have a feeling coming up inside you.

This feeling is not who you really are. It is like a storm passing overhead. The sky is not the storm; the earth is not the storm. The storm passes over, makes a lot of noise, and the sky eventually clears. You are the sky, expansive, limitless, and spacious. There is no end to who you are. And if you are to look at the sky it attaches to nothing. It doesn't grab onto the earth; it doesn't hold onto a tree branch shouting *'I must fix this storm'*. It simply is, there, always, calm, always still – as are you, the real you.

The moment you try to fix the feeling is the moment you are the sky trying to grab a hold of that branch. By stopping, watching while feeling, perhaps labelling gently, you are then the sky, open, radiant, ever watchful and expansive.

Sometimes you will have spent a long time attempting to do something 'good' with your life, something worthwhile. You may have had an idea about who you wanted to be, or perhaps a part of you feels this intense desire to prove your worth. Maybe you dabbled with lots of different projects, jobs, relationships, opportunities and nothing ever came of them. And because of your earlier upbringing, your earlier life trauma, you never believed you could ever make something of your life, or experience success in the outer world.

So you gave up trying, or you kept on trying but never quite completed a task. This was no mistake.

Sometimes you need to try and fail, try and fail, try and fail, until you come to a period in your life when the outer mirror of success that others are achieving is becoming so loud, so huge, that this intense rage you have been feeling grows, and this rage becomes your greatest gift. Your rage is a big signal that it's time for change.

You've come to a point in your life where you've held yourself back, you've decided that somewhere along the track of life there is simply no point in trying anymore, and you hear the do-gooders out there saying: *'If you don't try, nothing will change'*. And yet they have not experienced the same journey, or what feels like consistent failure in every project, everything you put your heart into, until there comes a point where the heart cannot hurt anymore and you stop and give up.

But then the gift of rage rears up inside you. This rage is the turning point, a swinging pendulum of change. At one end the pendulum swings to rage, and at the other end swings to contentment and relief. The rage begins to grow only when you're ready for a change in your life. It is not a bad thing; it is not a sign that you are failing or going backwards on your spiritual path or life journey. It is an alarm flashing: **It is time; it is your time now!**

People go through so many cycles in their lives. Those who suffer from depression may be in sadness, may be in anger, but when the rage comes, it will not stop coming until change happens. Rage means change. This may go against everything you have been taught, but if your life path has been littered with 'perceived failures and lost dreams', rage is your wakeup call and it is time to get up and look out and see: **What is here for me?**

There was a time in life when the people around you were gently showing you what was possible, and it niggled you as you felt unworthy, undeserving of a better way to live life.

And then more people came to show you how successful, how beautiful, how kind, how loving, how confident, how good they are at their careers, jobs, self-employment, relationships, and the numbers increased until you were surrounded by people living 'the dream'; the dream you had been desiring for so long, and something snapped inside - the rapids of rage.

The rapids of rage flow through you and set you on a course of turbulence in the beginning, where you need to face the boulders, the rocks, the dangers of the rapid feelings rising up within you. Until eventually you come to the end of the rapids and go over that waterfall, that big change, and tumble down, but you discover that you land safely in the water beneath you, as the raft carries you on, and the river bends and twists, and moments of calm, moments of sunshine, moments of beauty await you. All of this because rage knocked on your door.

Can you embrace this rage?

You can and will embrace this rage, because it will not stop until you surrender into the rapids of this emotion.

The hardest thing is to be kind to yourself as you are in rage, but it is essential. As rage arises, say to yourself:

'Welcome rage, I know you are here, you are not bad, you are helping me, thank you for this gift'.

Chapter 4

~Attachment to Outcomes~

It is easy to get lost in the daily irritations of comparing yourself with others. This constant battle can be incredibly tiresome. In the beginning most of what you understand is all in the intellect, but experiencing something is an entirely different matter. Knowing that life changes, that life moves and changes exactly when it needs to, often doesn't bring you any comfort when trapped in a cycle of 'wanting and desiring' instead of accepting and allowing 'what is'.

You get caught in a web of your own making. Your desire to be free of suffering, your desire to feel less restricted internally or externally, can make change seem extremely slow going.

You get trapped between two worlds. In the one world you see that life naturally evolves; life naturally expands, and that you naturally change and grow. You understand that nothing comes to you until it's time. And you know this is an incredibly freeing thought, a freeing feeling. But you live in another world, where you understand the freedom you desire, but a part of you doesn't believe or trust the natural way of the world and you still hang on, trying to make things different.

You try to be limitless; you try to be free; you try to let go of control; you try to trust. And all of these attempts are fruitless, because all of them are doing - not being. All of them are effort - not effortless. You are not yet ready to let go of your attachment to outcome; you are not yet ready to let go of the steering wheel of life and trust in the bigger picture, the natural flow of the river of your own life. And so you struggle against the current; you ride that raft down the rapids and use your paddle to try to steer away from boulders and away from what seems like the impending doom of the waterfall you are about to go over. Yet if you surrender to 'what is' the journey of your life becomes more a graceful flow than a struggle to control.

And how do you surrender?

How do you surrender when every cell of your being is screaming that your life is not working and that you need to do something to make it work? How do you surrender in that moment when jealousies, envy, doubt, rage, resentment all rise up inside you? You accept that you are resisting letting go; you accept that perhaps you are not yet ready to take your hands off the steering wheel; you accept this with kindness to who you are in the moment, being gentle and tender instead of beating yourself over the head with the *'Must hurry up, time is of the essence, everyone is passing me by'* train of thought.

You take a step back, a moment of pause, to breathe and look around. You look to see if you are getting caught up in the tidal wave of humanity also rushing to fix, to control their outer world. You slow right down and pause. You ask yourself what are you doing and why? Are you trying to win over others? Trying to outwit your competitors? Beat those who seem to be doing well? Prove others wrong?

What if stopping in the moment gave you exactly what you were searching for all along? Freedom.

Freedom doesn't mean you have a lot of money in the bank; freedom doesn't mean you have lots of time on your hands; freedom doesn't mean you have the perfect relationship, job or home. When you pause, give yourself that breathing space, allow yourself to be in that moment, you naturally feel this expansion inside that feels infinitely free, open and calm.

You do not give yourself enough moments. It is time this all changed. You may feel that if you slow down, if you take your eyes off the prize, the goal, the outcome, that it will pass you by. But what if the prize, the goal, the outcome was not what you wanted anyway? What if what you really wanted was a sense of value, a sense of worth and deserving? Yet, these things you were attached to could never bring this anyway, and are the biggest illusion created by your desire to belong, your desire for ease.

Some of you may feel that if you don't do something soon to change your life, you will be left by the roadside, alone, homeless and in despair. But is the despair not there as you reach and grapple to create or manifest your desires through your own effort and will? What happens if or when those things appear in your life? Joy? Peace? Or a temporary sense of relief?

What if it is relief from the wanting you have been craving for so long, not the outcome, but the relief from the constant wanting. This feeling that if you just fulfil x, y, z, you will feel better. Perhaps you will feel better, but only for a moment, and the wanting begins again.

Perhaps this moment is not only all that you have, but is the only place where relief can be found - consistent, freeing relief. Are you willing to take the risk and stop and slow down? Can you give yourself a break from racing to the finish line in life?

Don't worry about your age, you may be 20, 30, 40, 60, 70 or beyond. Life knows no limits. Life has no age. The tree goes through many seasons. It grows, flourishes, drops its leaves and retreats into itself in the winter to conserve energy. In each moment, being born and dying to the present moment. The tree doesn't worry that it will never make another flower or leaf if it doesn't hurry up, because it has been on this planet for a long time. It knows no time. Only humans define their experiences in relationship to time, and humans are here to transform this way of being back to 'no time'.

God, the universe, life, whatever name you give to the bigger picture, is experiencing itself through you as a human being. A journey from effortlessness, playfulness, freedom, to human doing, suffering and beyond. You can all return to the effortlessness, playfulness, freedom and being, by allowing your moment-by-moment experience, allowing your feelings of pain, suffering, rage, anger and envy to be felt, observed and tenderly allowed. No more self-beating, no more rushing against the tide, no more trying to steer that canoe, for life knows the way, always has and always will.

You can try to control or create your life experiences, but it's far better to surrender to the flow and allow life to give you the perfect moments for your soul to expand and grow. Often life brings you opportunities and experiences you may never have considered before, and provides you with new knowledge, wisdom and inspiration that you may have resisted by trying to control.

Being in the flow, you see that all your emotions are gifts, those you perceive to be 'bad' often being the greatest gifts, once you listen to what they have to say. You do this not through words, but through witnessing, through warmly holding a space for your humanity to be held and lovingly embraced.

Know that what you need to do, know and be will come to you at the exact time it needs to take place. No need to remember how, or find out why, as life takes care of itself once you allow it to. This is by far the hardest thing for you to take in.

You are taught that surrendering and letting go is like giving up and not participating in life. You are told that you must be 'doing' all of the time. Yet this constant doing is not what brings peace. It is in 'being human' that will bring peace. And this begins with all of you through grace and flow.

If what you are doing right now is not bringing you peace, stop what you are doing. If you are in a job that you hate and you feel unable to leave it, you can still stop in the moment anytime, be with the flow of your feelings that are bubbling up inside you. If the activities you choose are filling your time; are distracting you from being with these feelings, ask yourself why? And then make new choices.

What do you want and why do you want it? What is the real reason you want that job, that house, that relationship? What is the real reason that you are addicted to that chocolate, that drug; that drink? Can you face you, and let you be held with compassion even in the midst of pain and suffering? Allowing the jealousy, the 'life's unfair', the resentment and the rage to have your full presence and give it your full attention?

Are you willing to take the chance to choose a new way of living? If your way has not worked so far in bringing you a sense of freedom and peace, what have you got to lose to surrender and drop into life's flow, and allow?

Nothing.

Now is the only time you have.

Change is happening.

Give up your desire to control the world.

Chapter 5

~Embracing Imperfection~

People often live life as if they are running out of time, and yes, while the body eventually departs this world, it is not always necessary to be rushing. It's not the end of the world if you put off a task or action that you want to fulfil. The Earth will not stop spinning, nor will your personal world come to a standstill. Everything gets done when it needs to. And when I say everything, this does not mean everything on your 'to do' list of life.

Sometimes your list is the controlling factor causing you the most stress; the list of actions to be completed by the end of the day; the list of things to accomplish before you reach a certain age. These are all your need to control, to give you a sense of belonging and fitting in.

What if you were to allow imperfection into your world? What if that painting you hung on the wall was lopsided, that hair was out of place, you walked around with a big red dot on the end of your nose? What would actually happen in the scheme of things?

I know that for some of you it would feel very uncomfortable. You would sit on your sofa looking at that lopsided painting and feel this desperate need to get up and straighten it, yet can you not see that this is what you do to yourself all day long, every day of your life, when you are afraid to surrender and let go?

You rehearse what you are going to say to 'so and so' at work. You plan out in advance where you will go, what you will see when you go on vacation. Your planning, your controlling, your need to straighten that picture of life is an ongoing cause of stress and struggle in your inner world. Are you able to sit with imperfection? And in doing so see the perfection in it all?

The world is not going to end if you don't get everything done in your timeframe. What needs to be done will take place naturally from a calmer, more present state of being. You have this need to know. Uncertainty is not often embraced in your world.

If you need the outer world to be perfect for you to be happy or to feel more content, imagine what restrictions you are actually putting on your life, limiting the natural order and flow of the Divine moment.

By living life by condition, you are saying to yourself that you need to be perfect in order to be accepted by the world. If you were out of balance, lopsided, not completely perfect, then you would see yourself as not lovable or good enough.

Your outer world mirrors your inner world. How you view your outer world is how you view you, your inner world, the 'you' that needs your care, your attention, your compassion and your love.

Day-by-day, moment-by-moment, as you spend time in deep presence with you, allowing yourself to feel anger, to feel rage, to feel envy, to feel sadness, to feel fear and panic... the way your outer world looks to you will change. Nothing physically may have changed, but you will no longer be affected by events nearly as much. Your outer and inner worlds are very much interlinked. If you want to see your outer world change, you need to find a way of making peace with your inner world.

Sometimes life will give you temporary sickness, ill health, broken bones, all ways to slow you down. It is all a mental sickness. Mentally, you will not take your vice-like grip off the steering wheel. You move through life as if you are on a marathon run to the finishing line, never stopping, always finding something new to keep you in that mode. But eventually you choose to stop, or your body steps in and stops you in your tracks. Sometimes ill-health comes to make you embody your body, to become more present than you ever were before.

Your constant need for things to be perfect not only causes you stress, but it can hold you back in life. You may have ideas, dreams for your life; you may have projects and things you could be doing right now in the moment, yet your refusal to even begin them happens because you feel you need to be more perfect, more capable, better at whatever it is before you can do it.

There are many artists, writers, photographers, lovers, and creative people in this world who never climb from behind the rock they have been hiding behind.

It is easy to procrastinate. Excuses you make are big and lengthy.

'I will start when I get the right tools',
'When I have the money I will start the business',
'When I am physically well I will make love with my husband',
'I will start writing when I have a top notch computer',
'I will do graphic art when I get the right technology'.

The problem with all these excuses, that many unfulfilled people use, is 'Yes... but'.

That rock is safe; that rock allows no rejection, but it also allows no admiration or praise from the outer world. Your perfectionism keeps you stagnant, unwilling to listen to your heart's calling. 'Yes, buts' are so easy to make, but there is always something you can do that gives you the opportunity to meet your calling in life.

You may need money to start a business. You may need tools to write, to paint, to create, but you have hands, you have options. A writer simply needs a notepad and can use a free library or college computer. An artist simply needs a sketch pad and a pencil. A photographer does not need a fancy SLR camera to be a photographer.

You are already capable of all of these things, but if you are waiting for an easy way out from behind that rock, it's not going to come.

You don't create or write to be successful; you don't create or paint to be famous or to increase your wealth. You do all of these things because your soul is calling you to do them. If the most memorable artists of your time stopped at their first scribble, their first essay, their first sculpture, when it may have looked messy, may have sounded odd to them, they would never have had the opportunity to savour the beautiful unique creative landscape they chose to share with you all.

Are you that artist? Does your heart yearn to write? The question is: Do you want to be a painter or do you want to paint? Do you want to be a writer or do you want to write? The painter and the writer are all labels which your human ego needs so as to feel better, to feel important, to impress. Your soul, the universe, simply wants to paint, write or sculpt whatever 'it' is. The universe does not need to be a writer, although the labels help further down the line if you do publish your work, but this is not who you are.

You are an infinitely beautiful, unique version of source energy, and that energy creates - no limiting labels. Creative energy simply flows through your words, your art and your outlet; that is unique to you. Dare you miss that opportunity to spread that light? To share your life force?

Yes, it feels good to say *'I am a writer'*, *'I am a photographer'* etc...but, when you sit all alone with yourself in your quiet moments, who cares if you are a writer or a photographer? Who cares if you are famous or rich from your work?

Source is simply experiencing writing, flowing through the creative you.

What would it feel like to be ordinary? To embrace ordinariness? What if simply being you, and everyone else simply being who they are, is perfectly natural, perfectly ordinary, and in that ordinariness is the absolute perfection of the nature of this universe and reality?

Ordinary does not mean less than; ordinary does not mean your light does not shine. It simply means that you are content with who you are. You do not care for the labels of outstanding or brilliant. If you can be you, without needing to be someone special, and be not only okay with that, but feel good enough, this is real freedom. Your attachment to labels, attachment to perfection, and attachment to things being a certain way before you can be happy with your place in life, are gone.

I wonder, can you embrace being ordinary?

Chapter 6

~Change – Transition~

Human life can seem so frail, so limited on its journey. Change is a natural process that happens to all life forms. Change can feel very challenging to many, as its basis is that of great uncertainty, of the great unknown.

It can feel difficult to trust that all will be okay when change feels overwhelming. Sometimes change comes all of a sudden, sometimes it is expected. Even though change is expected, for example the change of a job or the move to a new home, it's still not an easy experience for many people.

Sometimes life changes in a way that you cannot humanly see how you are going to handle it. Perhaps you are evicted from your home, and you do not have the resources to move, put down a deposit or pay rent on a new place, or perhaps you lose your job and you have to take care of your family. This kind of change can be debilitating to the ego because it likes to be in charge, it likes to be in control, and this kind of change leaves the ego in chaos as it cannot control what is happening, or find a solution.

Death is similar. Losing a loved one is something totally out of your control, but all of life is out of your control. You cannot control change, you can only embrace it, accept it, and allow change to flow through you. Graceful surrender is the greatest gift you can give yourself during any time of overwhelming change. This is compassion, this is loving; this is the gift of the present moment.

Yes, the transition into the new can seem difficult and filled with fear and doubt; Yes it is out of your control how things evolve and transpire, but what you can do in these moments is to make the best of where you are, to not think too far ahead, but to be present and embrace the moment.

Change comes when you're ready. Even if you don't feel mentally or emotionally ready, something deep inside knows you are ready; it is time. Until this time comes you can choose to live each day, moment by moment, accepting, allowing and embracing what is. You can do nothing else, for you are not in control of the outer circumstances of your lives.

You may think you are in control; you may visualise, daydream and feel you are in control of what comes your way, but you never are. The efforts of the mind wanting to create your reality are simply food for the ego, not food for the soul. Food for the soul comes from the heart, comes from a sense of deep surrender, surrender to the flow of life, to what is, and allows change to naturally happen. To listen for the signs, to know who you are, so that when change comes around you are ready, and when you are ready you can make choices from your present moment awareness.

This is all you can do – surrender to grace.

You may feel empowered, feel you are in control, as you envision a better life for yourself, but whether it comes or not, being in the moment means that whatever comes is perfectly fine with who you are. Surrender enables a deep sense of grace, a deep sense of peace. You are then blessed by grace, blessed by surrender, blessed by faith and trust that all is well.

Something challenging comes; you are okay with it; something joyful arises; you feel blessed, yet you know that everything passes and moves through your life experience, always changing, never stagnant or stuck, so it fazes you less.

If you do choose to go down the route of trying to control or affect change by using affirmations, by trying to create a different future for yourself using visualisations, bear this in mind - do not be attached to what you envision, because what you envision may not be what is for your greatest growth.

Make sure you keep an inner state of flexibility, and are not tightly bound to your visions.

God, the Universe, Life, does not have tunnel vision, does not have only one door it wants you to walk through. Life is open, expansive like the sky, the ocean, the air you breathe. Don't limit yourself to a time-frame, or a shape for your life, this is the mind at work. Let your heart fall into deep surrender and grace.

Any natural visioning you have will be light, open and with no control involved. You may simply see something you would like one day and have a thought about owning it or doing it, a simple, light airy thought and feeling.

If it is for you it will manifest, if it isn't it won't.

Those things you have a 'desperate' yearning for are signalling through your emotions that it's not for your highest good to manifest them. It's not your heart's wanting but your ego's. Your emotions are a guide and can help you to see more clearly.

Your desire may not be in the shape or form that life wants to manifest through you.

So the emphasis must always be on ease.

Is it easy? Does it feel easy? Are the actions you are choosing to take easy?

If not, you may not be on the path of your soul. Roadblocks are messages from life to let go of the reins and to surrender into grace. Be open to change, to change that may totally surprise you, and be totally unexpected.

Chapter 7

~Flexibility~

It can be the bane of a human's life to hear that they must be flexible with their dreams. Some in the 'positive-thinking' culture will profess that anything is possible; if you dream it you can have it. But many of these teachings and messages bypass one relevant fact – you receive what you need and not necessarily what you want or think you need.

Many of these teachings can often create a culture of wanting - not allowing; attachment - not being receptive to what is perfect for your own joyful expansion and awareness.

Most people need to hear that they can have anything they want, absolutely anything! Yet to be told that they receive what they need - not what they want, often feels like a kick in the teeth, a blow to the ego, as being flexible and open to 'whatever is necessary' for their own soul growth can be a challenge to hear for many.

Those who may become wealthy or famous may need whatever the experience gives them, yet for another person also wanting that same thing; it may not be what they need in life for their own personal growth. Instead they may need to embrace a more simple life. Perhaps they have chosen to live from the heart and less from the mind, because at a soul level you cannot always know for certain what is right for your own growth. You can get hints along the way in the form of intuition and in the feelings you experience. You may feel something inside, about a path that would be good for you to take, and suddenly an opportunity or action becomes easy. Yet if you have desires and dreams that bring up fear; that give you a feeling of desperation, a real neediness and attachment to those desires, you may not be on the right path for your own growth.

You 'may' experience those things you want further down the path of life, but for now, or even for your lifetime, you may have other doorways to walk through, ones you had not even considered, and this is where flexibility comes in.

Are you able to open to the possibility that what you want is not what you need right now? If it was what you needed it would be in your life, right now, and it would come effortlessly.

If you feel you want to be rich and to have lots of money; if you desire this deeply, even go so far as imagining dollars floating through the air to you, and still many months on, or even years, nothing has changed in that area, you may have deeper needs to be fulfilled. Needs like awareness; needs like compassion towards yourself; needs to be more present and embracing what is and making the best of what you have and much more.

How flexible are you?

Sometimes you may have very little money and a burst of cash comes into your life and you think you definitely want to splash out and do something wonderful with it, go on holiday, or even just dine out at a fancy restaurant, but your partner may tell you, even with that inflow of cash, you are on a budget. You may feel disheartened, feel your fun is being stopped, but with a little flexibility and openness you can have a far better time by opening to using it in a wiser way, where the experience is more gracious and your partner may enjoy it more.

Flexibility in life is very important, in your choices, relationships and work. It is a surrender to the flow of life, without being attached to an outcome. Taking what is, and choosing the most uplifting option, the option that when with others, is not just a compromise, but a willingness to be flexible, and recognising that whatever happens is perfect in the scheme of things.

Flexibility is what the trees do when a storm comes, as the hurricane blows through a forest or town, the trees bend as the wind blows. They don't usually fall over like houses; they weather the storm because they have such strong roots. Their roots, like your own, are centered in the earth, centered in the abundance of nature, and being present and open is a way to strengthen your own root system, so that no matter what changes come in life you are not easily knocked over. You bend and are flexible to your own unique needs, those of growth, expansion and self-awareness.

Chapter 8

~Playing the Comparison Game~

There are times in your day when you feel 'less than' everyone else. The comparison junkie rears his or her head. People are prone to comparing who and where they are in life to others. This is something you do from an early age to distinguish between different and contrasting realities. It is meant simply so that you can see the unique expressions of life in your journey on planet Earth, but over time, through conditioned thinking, lessons taught through your culture, this is often turned into a full time job for the mind, and as a result it can be a total destroyer of self-worth and esteem.

To stop the comparison game can be challenging. It's hard to see someone living the life you desire and wondering why they have it and you don't. Perhaps someone seems more confident than you and socially connected as a result; perhaps someone appears physically prettier than you, richer than you, more talented, smarter than you, and this leads not only to envy and jealousy, but an intense resentment of that person. It is no longer about you. It's about pointing fingers and making judgments to make you feel better

This is a real experience for many. Sometimes you can see no other way to improve your mood, and so pointing fingers gives you a sense of temporary relief. But that is it, only temporary, and the feeling always returns, often stronger and more forceful with people shining so brightly you can no longer ignore them.

When this happens you have two choices. You can continue to resent them for having what you want, or, you can begin to change your understanding of what you think they have and you may also be able to begin to make steps in the direction of that life, and if it is for you it will begin to unravel and unfold.

If you see someone writing, publishing their book, and you sit and stew, feeling resentful that they are doing what you have wanted to do for a long time, but have not done, because of fear of failure or fear of success, this can breed hate and misguided resentment. Alternatively, you can start writing every day, even if it feels that it's not your best work, or it's not as good as the other person's, but once you begin, you will feel less insecure and more confident in who you are.

There will be days when you feel that what you are writing, painting, making, doing, is not very good and pointless. But you make a commitment to thirty minutes or more a day doing the very thing you think you are no good at doing. You do it to create, to let the energy of life flow through you. And now, that person you resented no longer causes you nearly as many problems. They may still push your buttons if suddenly a publisher takes them on and they become famous. Your ego will still niggle you, but instead of falling apart like in the past, and giving up because of this, you use this feeling to keep you going; you use it to feel more determined than ever to complete your creative project. The resentment becomes a gift, not a terrible thing traumatising you.

All these emotions that you're often taught are 'bad', emotions like anger, resentment, envy, jealousy, hate and rage are not bad at all. They may feel like the worst feelings on Earth, but once you begin to see the gift they are revealing to you, you will see the message in that dark feeling, that these were, and are, your biggest teachers all along.

So the next time someone brings home to you a feeling of intense envy and resentment, instead of becoming frustrated with who you are, or guilty for feeling other than happy that the other person is doing so well, soothe and comfort yourself in the knowledge that these feelings are here to stir you into some kind of change. They are not children who need to be chastised, or beaten and abused; they are children who need love and attention and your full presence, so that you can move through the feeling, knowing that it will pass. You can begin something new, and listen to your own wisdom speak through these human emotional reactions, and show yourself a greater kindness.

Your self-worth and self-esteem cannot be changed by doing positive affirmations. If that were the case many people would be super confident and are not. It may appear to work for some, but only because they have already faced the hurts inside that have caused low self-worth and low self-esteem, and are ready to feel differently.

Acknowledging the pain and the suffering that take place inside you, and allowing the feelings, will take time, but this new way of handling these feelings will change the way you relate to you and to the outside world.

The next time you feel something challenging, ask what needs your attention right now? Feel it and name it. This practice of being mindful has far-reaching rewards in life and in doing so you are saying: *'I am okay exactly as I am'.*

Chapter 9

~Being Driven~

A lot of things can drive the human being in a lifetime. Some may say that those who are less driven, more laid back, more going with the flow of life, are not only less driven, but less motivated.

Some people are born with a deep remembering of their life purpose and so can seem more driven, but all that has happened is that they are spontaneously flowing with the inner drive of life-force within them. But many are not born with this and it develops over time.

Comparing how driven you are with those who may have pre-chosen a life path of knowing early on who they are, and what they came to do, is fruitless, but it's often a challenge to stop comparing all the same. There are many people in their thirties, forties and into later years who have never experienced that strong drive because their life experiences needed to teach them, to bring out their innate wisdom, so that the strength of their purpose becomes clearer later on in life.

This purpose could be to be a teacher, but without a life of roadblocks, boulders and emotional turbulence, their teaching would be empty and void of any true substance. A teacher who has lived a life of ease and positive life experiences for most of their lives may teach upliftment to others on a similar path, but the teacher who has climbed many mountains, stumbled many times, and has had periods of heartache, can teach those who are struggling to recall who they are, and this is what is needed on this planet today.

A teacher does not only mean a writer, or a speaker. Someone can teach the local neighbourhood kids about kindness, acceptance and tolerance. An elderly man with a lifetime of experience can teach the wisdom of his wounds far better than a young man with few wounds and few life experiences. A mother is a teacher to her children. A road sweeper teaches that this Earth is valuable and deserves to be sparkling clean and blessed.

No life path is more or less worthy than any other. It's simply a matter of perspective and whether or not the ego judges and compares.

There are, however, some people who may seem driven, may seem assertive and empowered. They may set goals, appear emotionally 'together' and be strong individuals, but often this is not the case. What you see on the surface is not always what is taking place.

Being naturally driven from the heart, from an intuitive clarity, is different from someone who makes a list of what needs to be done, to get to a place they think they ought to be, and are using busy-ness to distract themselves from their inner world.

Being driven must come from a naturally spontaneous place, a place of surrender, a place of grace, no force, and no controlling desire to mould your outer world into what you feel it should be.

So the next time you compare, take a long hard look at the people in your world who appear to have it 'all together', but do they really? Are they simply doing what a large proportion of the world is doing; are they trying to control the flow of the river, trying through effort to make change happen?

Some may be naturally in the flow, and you will know. They will be easy to be around. Even if they are doing something you want to do in life, it will not irk you or irritate you, for their life force will be strongly present and strongly knowing. They will be coming from a different place.

Sometimes it can feel as if you are a kite just being blown about in the wind, tethered to the Earth, unable to fly free, but this can be viewed another way. You are rooted to this Earth, like the tree, and when it is time to spread those roots and acknowledge your worth, your purpose, and your own essential value, you will feel yourself let go and begin to trust. You will start to believe and have faith, but this can take time and this is why embracing the moment is so important to many of you right now.

You build houses to keep you safe, warm, and protected from the elements outside, but your own home is the present moment. Without the present moment it will feel as if you are being knocked about by all and sundry. Life events, people, circumstances, will no doubt floor you and give you a feeling of intense drama. Your life story will feel unsatisfying to you if you are unable to find a place within you that you can call home.

If you drive through life intent on making the next moment, the future moment a better one; if you have the belief that you'll be 'happy when', then this moment will never come. You cannot avoid this reality. **You cannot avoid the now.** It is your gift, it is your blessing, it is the answer you have been looking for to find relief, to feel blessed, to experience a more consistent inner peace and remembering. In the moment, you receive glimpses and awareness of who you really are. If you lead with the future in mind, you will miss a great opportunity to experience a sense of deep, long-lasting self-worth, and what life wants to give you.

This life is not a race.

Allow your own deep inner-knowing to experience this now moment.

Living day-to-day, moment-to-moment, can be a big threat to the organising and planning ego mind. The ego is necessary in that it encourages you to get out of bed in the morning, to get dressed and do what needs to be done in your daily lives. The ego encourages you also to make changes, even if this comes from an inner desire to feel better about who you are. Desires are not a bad thing, although they may feel that way, especially when they are unfulfilled. It's easy to judge desires that are not fulfilled, as a reflection of who you are as a person, as it brings out a feeling of unworthiness, of undeserving, and, most of all, simply not feeling good enough.

Feeling not good enough can stifle the unique gift you came here to share. As you sit down and decide to create that work of art, make that piece of music, you sit and you listen to the voices telling you that you are not good enough, that there is no point going further with your passion, and many of you stop. And yes, stopping is also not a bad thing to do.

Sometimes stopping is all part of the plan, all a part of your own life's journey. If you awoke one day and had the urge to climb on your motorbike, wanting to speed down the street at a hundred miles an hour, you may have a dangerous accident, so, something slowing you down, or stopping you in your tracks, could mean the difference between living or dying, and it's the same with your desires and your passions.

Your life-force wants you to grow; your life-force wants you to live a fulfilled and joyful life; your life-force wants you to embrace living in the present moment, and knows that you have unique talents and gifts for a reason. These talents and gifts are not only meant to be explored and encouraged, but they are meant to be expressed.

However, this does not mean your life will be full of smooth-sailing, flowing into the life of your future dreams. No, often life needs to give you the hurdles, the road bumps, the traffic jams, and the parachute on the back of that motorbike, to prevent you from taking a turn that would not be for your highest good. So those apparent failures, those mistakes, those starting things and not completing them, all have a reason and a purpose - to get you to where you are right now.

If you start something you are interested in and you stop, and then you start something else and you stop, and you do this many times over your life, this can often lead you to a new experience, a new doorway you had not even considered going through. Admittedly, some people choose to start and stop for an entire lifetime and this may be what their life experience is all about, for whatever reason, but for most of you, there comes a time when you realise it's time to focus, time to get busy and time to follow through on those passions that are wanting to be deeply expressed through you.

No stopping anymore, just steady progress. Sometimes slow steady progress, but progress all the same.

There will be many times as you take a step through the door of this new life path, and you keep persistent and focused on expressing your passion, where you have days and moments, sometimes weeks, where you simply feel you are just not good enough and so why bother? But, instead of as in your past, something inside you will be encouraging you forward, because this time something has shifted, and this time your life purpose needs to be expressed.

This is not like before when you had an attachment to something manifesting in a specific way. This is your life energy calling you forward; your life energy calling you out from behind that rock; your life-force needing you to reignite that passion, to allow and embrace what you came here to do, and this is simply the beginning.

In your moment-by-moment awareness, the time you spend being present with 'what is', you evolve into a new inner confidence, a new inner self-respect. You know that all those times of being slowed down, all those road bumps, traffic jams and parachutes holding you back, have knocked your confidence, and you realise now, that doing this, keeping committed, is the biggest gift you are giving yourself. It is the beginning of feeling good enough; it is one step on the path to worthiness and to deserving a life that you're ready to be living, in the moment, now.

This is when you catch up with the flow of your life stream. You will know when you have caught it and it is time, and you will know when it isn't. The key is to become more present, gentler with yourself and more appreciating of 'what is', if you don't yet feel ready to initiate change.

You'll be ready for this change - when you're ready – not a moment before.

Don't beat yourself up if you're not ready.

You may be in that cycle of life where your life energy is slowing you down for a greater opportunity, a greater opening, but for now, it's time to embrace where you are and let your life be what it is.

When it's time for your self-commitment, your ego will flood you with excuses and distractions, but this time you will walk past them. You may sit at your keyboard, ready to write and crave chocolate, and ordinarily you would go and get some chocolate and be distracted by the intake of a temporary fix, but now, instead, you say to yourself *'After I have written I will give myself a treat'*. These small changes are huge steps for you on your new pathway.

Appreciating these small changes gives you an inner feeling of self-respect. Before you committed and focused on making these changes, your rage, your resentment, your anger, may have been huge towards those who were living a life you desired, but as you start to take these steps, this lessens. Some days it may still pop up, but you feel better able to handle it, as you can now say to yourself: *'I am focused, I am committed, I am taking steps in expressing who I am.'*

Chapter 10

~Keep Your Passions Private~

One very important step to make as you begin changing and stepping into your passion, is to keep quiet about this passion. Mention it to one person, a loved one whom you know will give you one hundred per cent support and encouragement. But if you do not have a person like this in your life, don't mention it to anyone.

As you begin the creative process it is essential that you carry your new expression as a woman carries a baby; carry it in your creative womb; do not reveal it until it is ready to be birthed, and don't even say to friends you are painting again, or writing a book, or starting a business or anything. The temptation to do this is so great!

You will find that in your past where you feel you have failed, where you did not follow through, that you may have shared what you were doing with others. Some of you do this to slow your progress down. Something in you feels that nothing will ever work out for you and you know that if you share it with others you will not complete the project or creation. It's a kind of self-sabotage, but sometimes it's necessary, because the creation you may have been intending to birth may not have been the highest possible creative expression that can come through you at the time, and at a later date, like now, you could be even more ready.

And when this time comes, you know that it's a sacred creation, you know that it's not meant to be revealed until you are ready to give birth to it. And giving birth could mean putting your artwork in a gallery, putting your business online, or receiving your book back from a publisher who has giving you a contract to sell your book.

The sacredness in this change is significant.

By holding this close to your heart you are saying that this creation matters, this creation is not a failure or a mistake, this creation needs nurturing and your love, attention and focus until it is ready to be revealed. Keep this blessing close to your chest. Do not reveal it prematurely. Feed it with your care and your tenderness until it is time to birth it fully.

Chapter 11

~Anger and Blame~

In the beginning, as your life begins to unfold and change, it may seem to be doing so at a snail's pace. As you smell even a hint of change, you may begin to feel even more anger and frustration at those life events and people that bothered you before. If you want to move house, or leave a job, and you can see changes slowly taking place, a work colleague or neighbour may feel extremely annoying to you. This is a natural process, to project your inner challenges out into the world.

The neighbours, the work colleagues, the people you meet in your life are as big a gift as rage or envy. Before you began to be committed to your creation, your new beginning, the little things they said and did may have caused you to feel fury, rage, blame, extreme irritation and a major feeling of powerlessness. Feeling like a victim is common; feeling like a victim to circumstances.

But, as you begin to focus daily, take daily steps on your path, allowing yourself time to express your inner light, your inner message, your feelings will shift. Instead of the anger completely wearing you out, you may find you swear and cuss at the circumstances, perhaps still go into blame mode, but it does not last nearly as long. Your reactions lessen because you are beginning to feel more self-respect and self-value. Your confidence is slowly growing. You feel more appreciative of who you are as you experience slow steady progress, moment-by-moment.

As your boss criticizes you, or your neighbour turns his radio up loud, you embrace the moment, knowing that change is taking place and that you will not be in these same circumstances forever. You can see that instead of feeling powerless, you feel more empowered as you embrace and focus your passion into doing something that you love, no matter how small this something may be. It is a beginning and this makes you feel more grateful, more tolerant and accepting of life's gifts in the form of button pushers in your life.

The 'not feeling good enough' thoughts will become less as you step forward on your path with increased focus and commitment. You are giving yourself attention; you are giving yourself care and love by being more present; you are adding value to your creation.

Your creative energy is simply flowing out from within you now, and this opens the doorway to many other opportunities that will come your way, when it is time for these changes to take place.

These changes may come in the form of abundance; they may come in the form of job offers, friendships, or opportunities to learn and gain knowledge or a chance to experience kindness from a stranger or joy from a child.

Before, you may have not been ready to express your creative flow, and that too was perfect. The slowing down, the frustration, the feelings of failure, were all gifts. They helped you to be where you are now, ripe and open to change, ready to keep your heart open and allow an outpouring of your creative talents and skills into the world.

Your relationships with others, yourself and the way you relate to the world around you will begin to change as you step into your power.

Driven is no longer a word that feels controlling. You no longer have this need to control the way things work around you or manifest. Your natural day-by-day, present moment allowing, is taking care of all of this as you let your life force be expressed.

You know what to do and when to do it, because you are not forcing or willing change. Change is just coming to you, and you take the right steps in the moment. This is how life is supposed to work. As nature evolves, grows and changes, so do you. Your essential nature knows how to let go, surrender and allow life to flow through you effortlessly and graciously.

Let it happen.

You are that ever-expanding moment when you surrender; when you accept 'what is'; when you embrace the changes taking place, and when you trust in the divine plan taking place in your life journey

Your life has a natural motion. Surrendering reveals how flowing this life could be.

Chapter 12

~The Story of 'Not Good Enough'~

When the 'I am not good enough' tape is playing, this can feel frustrating, deeply frustrating. Because you know you want to feel good enough and you know you want to experience those things that other people experience. Sometimes you even feel betrayed by God if you believe in God, or let down by life. This is where allowing 'what is' and accepting 'what is' is essential to become the person you are here to be.

You could enter a competition to win a new television and while you are hopeful that you will win, beneath that is this story of 'not good enough' playing. You believe you have no chance of winning and you feel frustrated, angry at yourself for not feeling good enough, and raging at those people you perceive to be stealing your prize who perhaps do not need it as much as you do. Well, this is your perception anyway.

What if I were to say to you that those people who won needed that experience more than you? They may already have four or five widescreen televisions in their home, but somewhere deep inside they need another one.

Sounds preposterous doesn't it? And to some, the rage arises and the voice shouts: *'Just plain greedy if you ask me!'* Yet what if their entire life revolves around keeping up with the

Joneses, looking wealthy for the sake of appearances; what if their comparison junkie is actually bigger than yours, so much so that at a soul level they allow in that new TV? Would you swap their inner world for yours, if all they have is the material world to give them comfort? Take it all away and many of these people you perceive to be better off than you would be devastated. They would not know how to cope emotionally with what to them is a tragic loss.

What if I told you that you are far wealthier in your spirit and in your heart because you see that feeling good enough, feeling relief, feeling peace, experiencing an inner freedom is far more gratifying than the material world?

Would you see these people as stealing your prizes as better off in the long term? What about people who are so busy 24/7 non-stop doing, that they never take a moment to breathe. Their life is full of distractions, so that they don't have to hear or experience what they are really feeling? To you they seem successful, together, strong, assertive individuals, but what if they were so busy in order to stop themselves falling apart on the inside?

Your journey right now is coming from within. Your heart is opening and needs to experience so many things, even those things that seem *'not fair'* or *'why them, not me?'*. Those material things, relationships or opportunities that you want 'may' come, but when you become less reliant on them being in your life to give you peace, or enable you to feel blessed; when you stop needing anything in the sense of *'I will be happy when...'*; this is when those material and life changes may come to you, when they are light, naturally unfolding and do not give you the huge exciting fix you had been thinking they may give you all along. They come when it's simply a lovely sigh... sigh.. That is really nice!

The Story of 'Not Good Enough'

This is far more rewarding than running around screaming for that temporary excitable fix that many in this world now crave. The western world especially is a civilization of 'wanting' addicts. Their addiction of choice is wanting all the time.

Wanting is not a bad thing, but if it gets out of balance to the level of wanting all the time, and being very attached to the outcome, then it is an addiction, no different from drugs or alcohol, a need to fix what you feel you are missing inside. And the gift of presence, of coming home to you, in this moment, now, is all you have been seeking all along through the outer world.

No need to stop making plans, or organising your time, but doing all of this from the present moment, listening to your instincts and beginning to sense and hear your intuition. This inner guidance will always take you in the direction that is for your highest good; a direction of soul growth and soul expansion.

All humanity really desires deep down is to love, to experience feeling loved, and to be seen. This is what humans most often want from anything they desire deeply. When that love is found within your heart, you will then no longer need to prove yourself to anyone.

Chapter 13

~The Present Moment Is Never Dull~

Many people feel that if they stop for a moment, simply breathe and really feel where they are, it will be boring or dull. Some believe that without the excitement of future goals, future hopes and dreams, life will be depressing and sad, but this is so far from the truth. You still have hopes, you still have dreams, but you're no longer deeply attached to them.

The suffering is from unfulfilled outcomes, not unfulfilled dreams. It comes from the attachment, the inflexibility, the tunnel vision, the believing that there is only one way to go in life; the not being open to what could be even better than you could have ever imagined in your wildest dreams, because, what naturally unfolds brings a sense of sustainable, inner contentment.

It is not for the outer world to judge your worth or your value, for in being in the moment you know your value, you see and know your worth and you experience this more fully. Yes, it may take time; yes, it may take years to feel this consistently, but start today and you will not regret this life change.

Being present also means that if life is overwhelming, if you are in the midst of some major drama in your life, that you can also make the choice to use distractions consciously.

You are present enough to know what your needs are; you do not do this out of robotic distracting or fear; you are simply aware that you are not able to handle what is coming up right now and that you may need a break from the pain, or emotional self. And this too is okay. **Nothing is not okay.** You are a human being. What you choose is your choice; you can make a decision from many different places and in many different ways. Your emotional wellbeing is paramount.

Listen to your soul whispering to you today. It does so softly, it does so with love. Are you ready for this change?

Listening to someone is a great gift. Letting them know that they are here, now, and that you see them, that they are not invisible, can shine the light on many a weary heart and soul. Many humans boast and show off simply because they no longer wish to be invisible and they cannot see any other way to get the attention and the love they seek from within. Even if the attention is negative, it is attention all the same, for most humans crave to feel loved and to feel that they exist and that someone notices.

The crazy thing about all this is that once each person begins to make peace with who they are, in this moment, the more people will begin to notice them and the more their invisibility mask will wear off.

If you have been walking this life feeling invisible, feeling that you do not matter, feeling that you are simply not valuable or important in the scheme of things, you are wrong. Just because others do not see your value does not mean you are not of immense importance and value. The world is incomplete when you are not taking the stage of your life, but you will discover that allowing yourself to be 'whatever you are' in the moment, accepting your life as it is, you will begin to see that the outside world will notice your value, your worth, your important place in this universe.

It will come as a surprise when people suddenly comment on what a great support you have been, or say that you are an inspiration or that you comfort them greatly. In the beginning you will feel distant from that, as it seems alien to you, because to you, you have not changed your outer activities, you are simply being you.

You are respecting yourself more; you are believing in yourself more; you are taking time to be natural and spontaneous, allowing life to unfold through you. As you force less, control no more, allow the space in your moment to actually feel the moment being lived through you, the outer world halts to attention. **Suddenly your light is on.** People will see you, perhaps only as a flicker at first, but as you allow your inner strength to grow; as you allow yourself to be creative, in whatever way that means for you, and doing so without the need for outer attention until whatever it is, is birthed, you will seem noticeably different to others.

Friends and family who perhaps did not 'see' you before, and who you may have felt ignored you or who were not interested in what you said, did or experienced, will suddenly begin to take notice, pay attention and want to connect with you more than they ever did before.

You have a glow even though they will not be aware of it on a conscious level, but those around you will begin to be drawn to you, like moths to a flame.

This is what happens when you begin to live in the present moment – you are more visible. You have been a dormant seed for what can feel like decades to some of you, and now that seed has sprouted and your young leaves and stem are slowly emerging above the ground. And over time, as you continue to be present, regardless of what is happening in the moment, your stem will grow strong and your flowers will blossom as your buds begin to open.

Perfection is no longer something you wish to attain in life. **You simply want to be you, moment by moment.** Those dreams and desires you may have had many years ago, that you gave up because they were unfulfilled, seem so distant and empty to you, for they were there merely to fill a gaping hole which the present moment now fills for you.

Perhaps you wanted to travel the world for a lifetime, to be famous, to be rich. And you can now see how many of your dreams were a way to escape the hum-drum of what you experienced as your world and life. BUT, now you experience the vitality and vibrant quality of life in the present and you no longer have any need for empty dreams. You may still want to see the world and have greater abundance, but you have no attachment to the way in which any of these things take place, or if they take place. You find contentment and presence has gifted you more peace than you ever imagined was possible in your earlier life experiences.

"What hurts you, blesses you. Darkness is your candle."

— *Rumi*

Chapter 14

~Money and Wealth~

In this world today, there are many ways of looking at different life experiences. Some people see poverty as being the worst kind of experience to have. They see those living in slums, without money or food, as a life not worth living, but those same people can be so devoid of wealth, an inner sense of wealth, that they miss the opportunity for valuing life in all its shapes and forms.

There are people in your world so financially and materially rich that many people envy what they have. Yet take away their riches and you would see a shallow, empty and often depressed existence. On the other hand there are many people who have very little but who are very happy.

Others may see £10, £100, even a million pounds as a drop in the ocean in their life experiences. They lose their appreciation of what they have, and many of them fear losing it all, so they spend a lifetime trying to hold on to it. This is not richness of spirit or wealth. Wealth is a feeling, and to be rich with no appreciation or value placed on both outer and inner wealth is a lonely existence, a place where most people would not want to be.

It is easy to say *'Yes but, at least I can be miserable in comfort!'* but why not face and embrace your inner richness now? That way, when or if the outer wealth comes your way, you are in a state of deep appreciation, trusting the natural flow of change, not afraid you will lose it all, because you will have your own inner resource to draw on, your own inner light.

Nothing can cause you to be knocked over. You could be rich one day and poor the next (materially speaking), and while you may have some reactions, it would not destroy you, because you would not have your sense of who you are dependent on what you own, have or do in life.

It is natural to feel anger and yearning when people don't value what they've got, and just throw it in your face, flippantly devaluing what they have in front of those who are less fortunate. Yearning is a painful suffering to experience. Often those boasting about what they've got all the time have forgotten the true value of simply being.

They may measure their own value and worth by their status or what they have in life, and this too is as much suffering as yearning and attachment can be. Whereas you may be attached to manifesting certain experiences or opportunities into your world, they are attached to the material objects, status and power. Neither is better or worse, they are simply attachments that do not bring long lasting contentment.

This moment is the only place where true contentment is.

If you cannot experience the moment or embrace your circumstances now, when you have a lack of whatever you want (money, health, love, friendship etc.), this will not change when you acquire those things. Peace is an inside job and the outside is just icing on the cake and is not as important once you have faced your inner demons; your inner yearning; your inner wanting in this very moment, right now.

Can you want and feel that want without trying to get that want?

When the yearning is deep and painful, the gift in the present moment has been calling you home, your home here, in this moment, blessing you with its peace, its love, its serene quality and spaciousness.

The present moment is where love is.

At Christmas, if you celebrate this festive day, it can feel the most challenging time for those of you who may experience loneliness, who may experience a lack of money. You will walk around shopping malls and see all the bright shiny things and your cravings may be heightened. Your envy, jealousy and resentment peaks. You may wander around Christmas markets, see all the wonderful items, the delicious food for sale and see everyone buying and eating and drinking, and the yearning grows. Sometimes it can be hard to be in those situations as the feelings can be intense, but know that as you feel those feelings, you are doing the one thing that many people shopping are not. You are giving yourself the loving attention you need right now.

The material world can be a huge distraction from experiencing the peace within you. The need for romance, money and anything outside of you can be a huge distraction. Once you are fully in the moment, once you practice this daily, your moment will be so much fuller; so much more vibrant, and if your outer abundance increases, if your financial wealth increases, or you meet a new partner, or your health improves, or you move into a new home that you wanted, your heart will be full.

Not full with the outer stuff your ego thought it wanted, but full with the love you thought that all of those 'things' would give you all along. And the money, the romance, the house, is something you feel deeply appreciative of, but you know you are not any of those things. You are now so strongly rooted in self that change will not throw you or knock your sense of self anymore.

Do not get lost in creating your reality. If you want to get lost, get lost to the present moment, where you never lose your sense of self. Your ego likes to think it has the power to control your outer world, but it never did. Being fully present in your heart, in your body, in your now, you always had the ability to experience this world with contentment, peace and deep appreciation. Blessings have always been here, now.

'Not I'll be happy when......'.

Trying to create your reality is food for the ego. It is the controlling man's way, the one who is unwilling to surrender to the moment and trust in the grand design. You could try to create for an infinitely long time, but if your own life path is meant to be going in another direction, it would be completely fruitless. Your dreams and your desires are worthwhile – but only when you are not attached to the outcome and not basing your existence on what you can allow into your world in the future. Allow now.

Chapter 15

~The hard 'YES' and easy 'NO'~

If you were brought up in a culture where people wanted you to be a certain way, perhaps your family and your teachers at school encouraged this, but what you wanted to do was often frowned upon or discouraged. You may have built your identity around a false sense of self. This is when the common trait of people-pleasing begins.

In your early years, if your confidence was not high, if life had treated you unkindly, the only way to survive may have been to do what you could to fit in by pleasing others. However, as you grow and expand your understanding of who you are, you may want to break out of that mold, and you may need to begin the process of turning your *'Yes'* into *'No'*.

After a lifetime of saying *'Yes'* to others, saying *'No'* can feel incredibly challenging. You feel that if you say *'No'* that you will hurt another person, but what you really feel is that you will hurt the illusory you they have been seeing. If you say *'No'*, you risk people not liking the real you and this can feel traumatic for many.

The more in the moment you are, the more you begin to feel your intuition and inner guidance. You will find that situations or opportunities you may have said *'Yes'* to before, to keep the peace or to go along with someone, that your body responds with a jerk in your belly that tells you it is wrong for you to say 'Yes'. And so you begin to say 'No'.

In the beginning you may feel guilt for saying 'No' to someone, but once you practice saying 'No' moment-by-moment, you feel a great relief inside from listening to your intuition. Once the 'No' is said, suddenly a lightness takes place inside.

Consider your 'No' as a gift you can give both to yourself and to the other person.

'No' can mean you are saying 'Yes' to you.

It can also mean that you are saying I value myself; I value my time; I value my opinions and I respect who I am now. You are not responsible for how another person responds or reacts to your 'No'. Your 'No' could mean that they receive what they need in that moment, and you could be walking down a different road from normal and find an opportunity waiting for you that you missed by saying 'Yes' for too long.

The more you say 'No', the more life gives you reason to say a joyful 'Yes' to opportunities, change and life experiences. If you keep saying 'Yes' when you mean 'No', life will simply continue the cycle of giving you life experiences that keep you on the road you are on. Until you become present you may miss your inner signals.

You won't miss them forever. Eventually your current life experiences may become too painful and too hard that you have no choice but to say 'No'. But what a better time to say 'No' than when it is out of a more loving, empowering choice instead of feeling backed into the corner and choosing from there?

Your body is your guidance system; it speaks to you regularly if you will only pay attention and listen, taking time out to be present, to breathe into your feelings (whatever those feelings are), and allowing 'what is' to be. You hear and sense your inner guidance more strongly and you can experience the flow of life more gracefully.

Guilt is just an old reflex from people-pleasing patterns. You are not responsible for how another human being responds or reacts to your 'No'. Your life needs you to say 'Yes' to what feels good and 'No' to what doesn't. You deserve a life filled with positive 'Yes's and your 'No's also have great importance within these changes taking place.

If someone has become too dependent on you, and something inside you feels uncomfortable, it is time to say 'No' and give that person space to develop and experience their own intuition, their own inner strength. You are responsible for you and you alone.

Feel confident in your 'No'. Ride the waves of guilt in the beginning. This will pass, the more you embrace who you are. You are here to be you, not someone else's illusion of you. Break through those illusions now.

Your 'No' is loving to both you and the person you say 'No' to. It may not seem that way at first, but you must honour your own path and journey, and trust that life knows the way.

Beginning the path of your authentic self can sometimes feel mean to those around you at first. If friends and family have experienced you a certain way for a long time, becoming more honest, more opinionated, less likely to say 'Yes' to their wishes, they may indeed view you as grumpy or mean-spirited - let them. They need time to adjust to the 'real you' and you may find some friendships dissolving, if they were based on the illusion you had been showing the world. Let this go. It will be easier to have fewer friendships based on illusion as you allow your authentic self to blossom and flourish.

Sometimes it is better to have no friends than to surround yourself with people so that you feel lovable. You are lovable, valuable and worthwhile, regardless of how many friends you have or how much you socialize in life. As you begin to value your own presence, your own gifts, wisdom and understanding, people who like the 'real you' will want to spend time with you, regardless of how many times you say 'No' or 'Yes'. They will like this about you, your authentic nature.

If a cat tried to be a dog it would look strange, sound strange and behave strangely. You would think there was something wrong with it, and this is how many of you can feel when you have been living a false persona for a long time, as if there is something wrong with you because you are not being who you actually are.

As you step into your power, the power in the now moment, allowing what is, embracing your feelings, you will feel a sense of freedom being able to let friendships go, and to also not be afraid of people letting you go, or rejecting you, because you are different from how they saw you.

If you can be willing to walk away from any unfulfilling circumstance or friendship - you are free. Freedom is a feeling, not being afraid that something will happen if you do not have a sense of belonging, or the norm of lots of friends. It is not because you are unlovable, or that people do not like the real you. It simply means you need time to adjust to being who you are, and over time the world will mirror your confidence and comfort in being the whole of who you are, not the illusion you had been projecting all this time.

You may all know people who could not give a damn, genuinely do not care what other people think, and most of you admire this quality in them, and people seem to flock around them because they have no attachments to needing to belong, or needing people to love or like them. These people know full well that not everyone is going to like or love them. Some people will love them and like them, some will hate them and some will fall somewhere in between with a feeling of indifference. This is how the human personality works. You have preferences in what you like in a person but none is better nor worse than any other.

When you were at school you may have wanted to be part of the coolest group in school, the pretty women, the good looking and confident guys, but they just reflected this false perfection you had started to believe in from an early age as you were drawn into the comparison game during childhood. Now, as you drop the need for perfection, drop the need to be a certain someone so that the world approves of you, you will discover that the world likes you just as you are, and you are doing your life a disservice to be anything but your authentic self.

You will find in the beginning that you will not be able to be authentic with everyone. For example you may have strong interests in physics or spirituality and your family doesn't. You could sit with them for hours trying to communicate your interests and it would be rebuffed, ignored and people would simply zone out. So you can authentically accept that being authentic does not always mean sharing all of who you are with everyone. You simply choose to spend less time with those you are less able to be yourself among.

Every time you say what you want and what you do not want to others, you are saying that you matter. This is your self-value beginning to flow through you. So being authentic, letting the 'No's come, allows the changing nature of the universe to live through you. You are worthy of this flow; you are worthy of this grace; you are worthy of this ease and presence.

You are on earth to live your vision, to step into your authentic power, to feel the freedom in the flow of life's greatest grace. Your life is calling you now.

Chapter 16

~Change and a Sense of Urgency~

Don't be so hard on yourself when you are not changing fast enough. Your ego loves speed, is addicted to pushing and forcing things to happen.

Any sense of urgency is always the ego; any sense of grace and flow is always your soul. In the winter you may see buds on trees and the tree does not shout at the buds to hurry up and unfold, hurry up and blossom. No, the tree allows its branches to flower when they are ready, when spring comes and the tree blossoms are able to handle the weather and need more sun and more nutrients from the soil.

In the winter the tree drops its leaves so that any nutrients coming from the soil come through the roots into the strong trunk and base of the tree, which helps it handle and exist throughout the harsh winter and snowfall.

Your life comes in cycles, just like nature, so in a winter period of your life, it may feel like nothing is moving or changing, but a lot is changing underneath the surface of your conscious mind.

You have your own buds growing and readying themselves for the shift in your life season and change. And just like the tree, shouting at your own growth is not going to make you flower and blossom any sooner. It is a waste of time trying to force change and growth before you are ready.

If you blossomed before you were ready, just like the tree, your blossoms would die, not reach their full potential.

It would not be a sustainable growth; it would be a temporary feeling, and gone in the blink of an eye. It is far more worthwhile to practice patience, flexibility and to know that you will change and grow as you drop into your own natural flow.

Comparing yourself with others who may appear to be further along the path than you, or who are doing something you are wanting to but are unable to right now, is fruitless. They may be in a summer and you in a winter. You all go through seasonal changes; even those who appear to be achieving great outer success will meet a winter at some stage.

The only thing you can ever be certain of is change. Accepting that change comes and goes, abundance comes in, abundance goes out, and accepting the flow and cycle you are in, can help you to avoid forcing your will onto the outer manifestation of your world and life.

If you are in winter, you can rest more, go within, breathe into your feelings, experience your moments. If you are in summer you can be more naturally active, achieving things, doing things, yet all of these activities need to come from a present moment awareness, which is your strong base. Your roots are steady and your growth and expansion is sustainable.

Mirror your natural world, and allow yourself to drop into the season. Slow outer progress is necessary while greater inner changes take place, often without you realising. This can be a rewarding and far more graceful experience than putting excess effort into something you have no control over.

Let life be your teacher. Let life show you the way.

Chapter 17

~Judging Others, Offering Solutions~

It can seem very easy to look at other people and see what they need to do to change their world and life. It may look painfully obvious, that if someone is drowning in a sea of negativity, criticising themselves and the world and expecting the worst, they need to change their mindset. But this is not always the case.

You can never know what another human being needs for them to grow and expand in life. You are not able to set even a pinky toe into the life of another person, or feel their personal experience in any way that enables you to make a decision about what is best for them. You have not lived their life story, their history, their upbringing, their childhood, their school years, their friendships, their pain, their suffering, their losses or their fears. It is pretty arrogant to think you know what they need, but most of you still do this.

It is hard not to want to tell someone that they need to do X, Y, Z to change their world and to release their suffering. If you are not fully balanced in your wiser self, how can you offer any advice to another? The need to help another can sometimes be a distraction from your own self-healing. To want to heal the world, to make your life's work to help others, if it is coming from the small self, the ego, even if it comes in the back door of spiritual teachings, it does not mean it is the right thing to do for someone else.

Someone once said that if Hitler was in a room many years ago as a baby would you go in and kill the baby? The answer is no. You can never know the repercussions of such an act. Nature abhors a vacuum, so if the world needed a dictator for whatever reason, another would have filled his boots so to speak. You cannot mess with the divine plan, which takes place naturally and in the flow. You can never force someone to do something that is not for them, even if it is well meaning and trying to keep them out of emotional or physical harm's way. They must always be free to make their own decisions and choices in life.

How many of you feel you know what's best for someone else? Most people at some point in their lives have felt this way. Yet if someone comes to you and forces their opinions or beliefs about what they think you should do, and it is unwanted and not asked for, most people tend to feel pretty angry and upset about it, so why do it?

Everyone wants to be seen.

Everyone wants to be understood.

Everyone wants to be loved.

Everyone wants to love.

Can you begin to see the natural flow of the universe? Can you see that every little thing is perfect in its imperfection, even those things you would rather were different? You can never know why something is a certain way for someone. All you can do is embrace this very moment and be a good friend by accepting the continuous changing nature of your world.

Chapter 18

~It May Be Right for You...But~

It is easy when on the spiritual path or a path of self-development to begin to feel that everyone needs to know what you know or do what you do. As you continue to grow and expand and to remember your soul's calling, you will begin to see that guidance, suggestions, offerings, unless requested by another, are often not what that person needs right now. It is easy to get on one's high horse and become preachy, especially if the small self has you believing that what you are doing is better and more enlightened than what anyone else is doing.

Life is a great mirror also, in that those who push your buttons the most are often reflecting those traits that you are unwilling to own. For example, feeling someone is preachy and playing the Good Samaritan can be a common trait in spiritual circles, where it is seen as good to be a certain way. If you know someone like this who preaches what they do, the good they do in the world and then encourages everyone around them to do the same and it really pushes your buttons, lift that mirror up now. Somewhere inside you is a preacher, someone who believes they know what is best for others and what others need to do to better their lives.

The small self needs to be right, and in the process of trying to make itself right needs to make others wrong. Most people do this, if they are honest. Unless the person has no buttons to be pushed, has a sense of deep calm and acceptance within, most people still need to prove their worth through projecting outwardly.

Go easy on yourself.

You are learning, unfolding and unravelling decades of programming. You are not going to be a peaceful Buddha, without judgments, attachment or fear, immediately - if ever. You may experience moments of understanding, and gravitate towards peace and more loving compassionate ways of being, but in the beginning you are going to have your buttons pushed and these people are wondrous gifts here to reveal to you what it is that needs your attention and love right now.

No need to beat yourself up thinking that you have taken two steps forward and ten back. You have not gone back in your own spiritual growth; you are simply becoming more aware. In the past you may have not seen the traits that pushed your buttons so clearly, but as you release what is no longer working and become more present, you will have your buttons pushed even more as your inner mirror is polished and life reflects back at you any smears that are no longer working for you as you grow and change. These feelings coming up need your loving attention now.

Any suffering arising needs to be welcomed. You can care for your suffering by being willing to allow it fully, and cradle it gently within your heart, breathing deeply, as this too will pass, but for now it is coming up for a reason. Be willing to hold it in your heart and to surrender to 'what is', for what is going on within you is happening for a reason. As you become more centred in the moment, your responses and reactions to outer experiences will shift and change, and your honesty with self and others will have ripple effects outwards and inwards also.

Gentleness and kindness to that frail ego is so important. Yes, in the beginning you may continue to react and regret your reactions, but over time this will change; new responses will come in as you embrace these feelings, and know it is not a bad thing but a strong trait to allow yourself to be vulnerable in the interim period.

Chapter 19

~You Need Not Be A Saint~

As you share your inspiration, as you care for others' wellbeing, as your heart opens to your own compassion and wisdom, it may feel wrong that others praise you as kind, generous and a great person. For you can see inside your own mind that you can still be cruel and judgmental and a part of you is not able to take the praise or receive it fully.

Somewhere in your childhood someone somewhere told you that you were a bad person for having challenging emotions and expressing them. If you were critical, judgmental, angry or sad; if any of these emotions were said to be what a bad child has, you may find it hard to accept honest praise as your heart opens and you embrace the moment. The small self still judges, but there is no good or bad in you as a human, you are simply a human being. Good and bad are labels.

Just because you may have human reactions to outer circumstances doesn't mean you are not spiritual or that you are a bad person, far from it. You need not be saintly on the spiritual path to be a valuable worthwhile and deserving human being. If you were meant to be saintly you would be a saint and you would not be in human form. Instead you would be in the infinite light of spirit, of source energy, where there are no defining characteristics, only limitless love.

You came here to express that love through your unique human self and this includes ALL emotional patterns and traits.

You need not be a saint.

You are not a saint.

It's okay not to be saintly.

It's okay not to be 'good'.

It's okay not to be 'bad'.

It's okay not to be perfect.

What you are, right now, in this moment is okay, more than okay, it's who you are.

Chapter 20

~Feeling A Sense Of Not Belonging~

The majority of the world is led by time. Lives are tidily organised into events such as birthdays, anniversaries, Valentine's Day, Easter, Mother's Day, Father's Day, Christmas, Hanukah, The Festival of Lights... the list is long. And while these days may be meaningful to many, once you begin to spend more time in the present moment, they will have less of an emphasis placed on them. This is because you will begin to experience the sacredness in every day, in each moment, and no one day is more important than any other day to you.

In the beginning, for the ego, the small self, this will be a challenge. For when Christmas turns into 'Groundhog Day' and you see the same events taking place, the same music, same conversation, same programs on television, the same family dramas taking place and nothing new, it will bring about a feeling of detachment from the world around you.

As you begin to fully embrace the moment, it will not affect you in an uncomfortable way, but in the beginning there may be a fight between the old way of being and the new way. The 'old you' will want to belong; the old you will want to have expectations for Christmas; the old you will want to plan a great day - ahead of time. But the 'new you' will make it so that you can't even do this with the 'oomph' and excitement you did in previous years. The new you will simply not understand why everyone is so excited about one day.

For those of you who are alone, or who are simply doing nothing special, it is simply another day. The ego may fight against this and compare your experience with others enjoying parties, togetherness, community, and connection with people in their world.

Yet deep down they cannot be compared, for many people will be left with debt after Christmas and experience deep January blues, mainly because they placed all their exciting eggs into one basket – Christmas Day. If they are not religious the sacred will have taken a backseat.

Reward yourself on these global events, where a lot of people are celebrating; reward yourself with a moment in your day to feel those feelings. Allow the emotions of disconnection, longing, loneliness to be held inside your heart, and then care for the suffering that may arise. The more you are able to do this, the easier it will be to become more present and to allow yourself the alternative of not fantasising so much.

Chapter 21

~Loneliness~

Life always knows the way. If you are ready to really embrace where you are, 'what is' and how you feel, life will remove any distractions by removing people from your life.

Life is encouraging you to begin the process of be-friending you and this means first making friends and peace with your suffering. While you may miss socialising and the camaraderie of people in your world, the isolation can be a great gift leading you home to who you truly are, because within you is a whole world of love, of resourcefulness, of peace and presence, and once you tap into this you will not feel the longing for company in the same way again.

Your attachments to needing others to fill that void will be gone, for that void will naturally overflow with a deep sense of oneness with all life, not just humans, but the trees, the earth, the air you breathe, and your heart will open and begin to reach out in unconditionally loving ways to the world outside you.

Sometimes you will feel a longing to go out and do something fun, and you will long for company, someone to talk to, to engage with, socialise with, but no-one you know is open to that. There is a very good reason for this.

If you have friends who are not into intimate connection, it is because you are being challenged by life to find that intimate connection with your own inner being. Once your inner connection opens and strengthens there will be less of a need for others.

The other people in your world will be a blessing in your life, yet you will not feel lonely when they are not there and you will not feel needy for company anymore. They will want to spend time with you because the more present and centered in your heart you become, the less you will need them.

Your completeness is found within; it always was and always will be.

Outside events, people, material possessions, can never fill you or take away your suffering. It may seem to take it away temporarily, but it will always return until you have begun to make peace with you, with all of you. The suffering is your child, awaiting your comforting arms and heart.

Begin by compassionately caring for that suffering and you will experience a new found connection with the world outside of you.

As you begin to realise that suffering is collective, and that you are not the only one feeling the same feelings, you will no longer feel so alone. The collective longing for connection awakens in your heart as you are now willing to face and embrace the feelings coming up inside you.

It is only difficult, this feeling of loneliness, when you compare your outer world with others, but remember, the outer world of others is only a mask for what is going on inside them.

Loneliness

So many people have messy inner houses and you are comparing yourself with a mirage of reality that is taking place.

Be gentle with you; allow yourself these moments of grace as the pain is deeply embraced.

Chapter 22

~Judgements Are Natural~

If you made no judgements, you would make no decisions and have no preferences.

Judgments are a way to compare and contrast what works for you with what doesn't. It is easy when you are beginning to evolve and grow and have a desire to be more peaceful, calmer and more loving, to judge yourself greatly for judging others and the world around you. It is easy to judge your neighbour and then judge yourself for judging. This is a double-barrelled gun.

And then some of you judge spiritual people for judging, as if being spiritual means you will not have any judgments anymore. This is simply not true.

The wars are not taking place outside of you. Iraq, Afghanistan, wars among people, tribes, these are nothing in comparison to the number of wars taking place inside people on this planet today. No wonder so many of you are so exhausted, because you beat yourself up and attack your judgments daily. If you simply judged, accepted that you judged, did not judge yourself for judging others, the judgments would weaken and lessen over time.

Resisting your own value judgments actually increases the likelihood of them continuing and growing in magnitude.

The more you let go of the world you once knew and begin to embrace and accept 'what is' in your life, in the beginning your judgments and intolerance will grow, not lessen. It may seem natural to think that if you become more present, more centered in the present moment, you will suddenly become more tolerant and see with only eyes of love, but this is not the case in the beginning. As you sit with 'what is', what's within you will come out louder. You just did not hear it so loudly before because you were distracted by future dreams, by addictions and any distractions you could find to stop you feeling what was taking place within you.

Do not beat yourself up for your intolerance.

Do not beat yourself up for your judgments.

Do not beat yourself up for your rage and your anger towards the world around you.

Surrender and allow your inner world to evolve and change naturally. Bless those judgments and emotions. They are gifts highlighting to you a world within that is now receiving your focus and attention, and over time, with your love and care, it will be easier to embrace those aspects of you that were hidden for so long by life's distractions.

You are not a bad person because you judged your neighbour, your friend, a family member or a stranger.

You cannot allow kindness to flow through you until you allow yourself to be who you are in the moment. Tend to your own inner world, not that of others. If someone appears to be doing something that is not working and you feel the urge to grab them by the neck and scream at them *'Do it this way!!'*

refrain from doing so. It is not their inner world you need to make peace with, it is yours. Your urgent and demanding ways, trying to make others change, is merely your own inner frustration with your perceived inability to change yourself in the way you feel you ought to be changing right now.

But there is no 'ought to' in change. You will change as and when it is time for you to change, as and when you are ready for change, not a moment before.

Gentleness is key right now. Be gentle with the sore tender parts of you coming up to be heard as your focus is on the present moment, on those long lost hidden afraid parts of you, ready for your loving gentle focus and attention as you surrender to 'what really is'.

Chapter 23

~Inner Storm, Raging Thunder~

Some days, as you give focused attention on being more present, a tidal wave of rage will hit you out of nowhere. This may come as a complete shock, but it has been lingering and hiding, masked behind any distractions. Someone will do something or not do something and suddenly you feel engulfed in this thunderous roar!

There is nothing you can do in the intenseness of this hurricane feeling. All you can do is weather the storm, let it pass, express it verbally out loud, to yourself (not others) if able, or write down the exact feelings as they come up. There is no need to limit your speech, or be kind to others as you express this within the safety of your home or another safe space. You can let all of the judgments, anger, resentment, hatred be written out. None of this makes you a bad person, far from it. You are now willing to face and embrace this suffering coming to the surface.

Until you are prepared to bear witness to this suffering and acknowledge what it is, nothing can change. What is it deep down that is causing you the most suffering during this storm? Do you feel let down by life? Is life not fair? Are people taking advantage of you? Does it feel as if God has abandoned you?

Write it down, shout it out, and if this intenseness is too much and you have been feeling depressed for some time, seek out professional help. You cannot always work through this suffering alone. Sometimes being deeply present when the depression is so dark and cold can cause us to linger there instead of embracing and moving through the pain, so seek help if you feel you need to.

Sometimes the road seems dark and then, the raging storm comes to clear away the obstacles in your path. Sometimes to know your own worth, you need to express what you will no longer accept in your life. If you have spent one too many times feeling walked over by others; one too many times making the effort when friends do not, the rage has come as a reminder that you are worth far more than you give yourself credit for. You are worthy of friends who want to spend time with you; you are worthy of being treated well and being appreciated.

The rage is a gift literally screaming at you:

'YOU ARE ENOUGH! AND YOU ARE WORTH MORE THAN YOU ARE CURRENTLY EXPERIENCING!'

As the storm begins to break and you see a glimmer of sky peeking through, you begin to realise the great gift the emotion of rage is showing you now. Instead of feeling swamped or overwhelmed by it; instead of feeling that there is something wrong with you because rage is sweeping through your inner world, you see that rage is that strong self-assured, confident, loving, mother within you telling you, you are okay, you are enough, you are worthy and you are valuable.

Not when you are fixed; not when you are fully healed; not when you are kind and peaceful, but right now with all the anger, rage, sadness, fear, judgments, envy, and blame. Right now, deep inside your core you are a good person, not a bad person. You have love within you always shining out. Even at your darkest moments help is at hand. Your feelings are not to be resisted or feared; your feelings are not to be washed away by positively thinking your way out of a tricky emotion; your feelings are your guide; your feelings are your gift; your feelings are here to teach the greatest lesson of all.

YOU ARE ENOUGH – EXACTLY AS YOU ARE! RIGHT NOW.

The storm will pass. Ride it as it comes through. Soon there will be clear sky again. Bless the inner storms that take place for they are treasures not mistakes.

Chapter 24

~Don't Be an Island, Relationships Matter~

The spiritual path, especially for those who practice meditation, can feel solitary sometimes. As you begin to explore your feelings and your inner world more; as you begin to embrace your pain, your suffering with the tender arms of love, and your attitude and way of looking at the world, you may need some time away from society and what you were once immersed in.

The path of solitude brings great rewards, as the normal everyday distractions are removed and you are left with a space which only source within can fill; no outer drama to distract you from offering love to your pain. You overflow with feelings, and you recognise these times as a gift.

However, as time goes on, the solitude can become a prison, because in every life a balance is needed. And while there are immense gifts in solitude, there are also gifts to be found in relationships, relating to people, be it friendships, with strangers and/or family. Dropping your guard, allowing your vulnerability to shine out, and letting yourself be not only seen but felt, and held in the arms of your human community, is an essential part of the spiritual journey also.

If you have spent many years alone, embracing your feelings with solitude, there comes a time when part of the feelings emerging are those of a longing to reconnect with humanity, and if you can discover and find one friend or person to open yourself to, this can be a great blessing. Often, many of your feelings and sufferings relate to past hurts and pain related to other people too, and to heal this pain you must involve and integrate yourself back into the community.

Through honesty and authenticity you can make changes. Allow yourself to unlock your heart and take the risk to be truly seen, and as you do, you will see more clearly. The heart needs to open and relationships are great triggers.

If you come across a teacher or guide who is willing to hold you in unconditional acceptance and understanding, this gift can be immense. In time you may be able to offer this same gift to others. To be raw and tender can not only open your own heart to self-compassion, but your vulnerability gives others in your world permission to be raw and vulnerable also.

Everyone simply wants to be loved, to be held, to be seen and to love. This is being human.

Chapter 25

~Too Much Emphasis On Positive Thinking May Damage Self-Worth~

There is a train of thought that positive thinking is of prime importance if you want to be a better person, have your life change, and be a valuable member of society. Some feel that positive thinking creates your reality; some believe that positive thinking is the only way to success. Many of those following this route view negative thinking as bad, wrong and a terrible waste of time and energy, and some can be almost evangelical in their views of being positive versus being negative.

For anyone who has experienced depression, anxiety or intense loss of any kind, they will know that being positive does not always right all wrongs. And sometimes if someone has a deeper, more challenging inner world, then to simply tell them to change their thinking to a more positive mindset is equal to saying to someone who is seriously depressed, *'Cheer up, it may never happen!'*.

Anyone who has suffered depression knows how much of a kick in the teeth it can be to experience such a lack of understanding and compassion for the human emotional journey.

No! Positive thinking when embracing the moment is a by-product of naturally allowing, of naturally accepting and acknowledging the present moment experience – whatever that may be. Positive thinking need not be a forced unnatural thing like reciting affirmations in front of the mirror. No! Positive thinking is simply the other side of negative thinking; where there is yin there is yang; where there is feminine there is also masculine; where there is comfort there is discomfort etc. etc... Once you begin to allow your entire human rainbow of emotions, then peace and freedom come more naturally. Forcing anyone to try to feel or think in a way that they are not able to, simply pushes the negative in deeper; pushes the discomfort in so far that it intensifies. So the positive thinking movement has its flaws, as does solely focusing on the negative in life.

From an early age you were taught to be and do in a way that is not natural for you. For example, children are expected from a young age to say *'Please'* and *'Thank you'*, and are often taught to express gratitude when they are not naturally geared up for it at such a young age.

Many adults don't feel gratitude until much later, so why expect children to fake an emotion they do not feel? This is the beginning of conditioning children to say *'Yes'* when they mean *'No'*, and can begin a cycle of self-esteem issues, as they do not trust their own feelings, but those of authority figures in their lives.

Positive thinking is the same in adults. If it is not coming naturally and the emotion is dark, heavy, sad or frustrated, do not try to be positive. Far better to sit for a moment, take a few deeper breaths, sense where the emotion is in your body, and simply watch it and feel it as an observer. It will not feel easy. This does not mean you will suddenly feel super happy.

It means you are not fighting yourself anymore. And the more you do this, the more space opens up within you for a more positive mindset. Your thoughts naturally change as you begin to accept yourself, and as you accept yourself more and more, you can accept the flaws you perceive in others, and life becomes richer and more meaningful to you.

Your human self deserves your love and affection. You did not come here to be less human; you came here to be fully human, a balanced human. Your spiritual self, your soul, is not urging you to be some angelic presence all glowing with only love and peace.

If this were the case you would never have chosen the earth plane to evolve and grow. Instead you would have chosen to stay as spiritual energy, limitless light, without unique expression or identity, one with 'all that is'.

No, instead you came here to be human. What greater love is there than to be fully your human self, the body, the experiences you chose to experience, the life you chose to lead, the awakenings you chose to awaken to. Your human self deserves so much more than you give it credit for. The spiritual teachers of the past, the wise sages, never advocated eliminating your human flaws, but embracing them and making them part of your inner gifts, talents and wisdom.

If a teaching leans more towards just awakening and encouraging only positive emotions like peace, love and gratitude, you are missing the entire spectrum of human feelings. From rage, peace can be found. In anger there is love lurking in the background.

All these so called 'negative' emotions are your greatest teachers, albeit feeling like your greatest obstacles at times. You can no longer bypass these strong emotions, but move lovingly through them, practicing loving kindness by allowing yourself to feel them, as if they were your children needing your tenderness, focus, care and attention, for this is all they are, aspects of you wanting to come home.

Chapter 26

~Falling Into Deep Surrender~

The world needs you to believe that to be happy you need to be 'doing' as everyone else is. The world needs you to fall in line with what is believed to be the 'perceived' norm.

When I say world, I do not mean the planet. The planet needs nothing from you. It is your grandest and most amazing teacher, blessing you with its spirit, its abundant life and its beauty. When I say the world I mean the societal structure that is man-made.

The difficulty arises when the world says that to be happy you need x, y, z, and then you realise you are not happy - it did not work. Christmas is a good example of this societal conditioning. Many in the western world believe they must be happy or merry at Christmas. The songs played on the radio speak of everyone being happy and merry. If you are not happy and merry at this time you are instantly an outsider and many people fake happiness via social media to feel a sense of belonging, but if they were really honest, they would know that they were not happy, that they were over full from food, alcohol and the addictive buzz of excitement through gift giving and receiving. Not the sacred experience of giving, the open heart, the genuine feeling of sharing. Too many are lost in the domain of materialism, overcompensating by gifting too much, or far beyond their financial means.

Many of you will remember as children your gifts may have looked large or you perhaps did not get anything. But now the pressure to conform and keep up with the Joneses has become so intense, because of sites like Facebook which are becoming places of mass illusion, that parents get mountains of presents for their children at Christmas, over compensating for something they feel is lacking. What is lacking is not gifts in the form of presents but 'presence'.

Presence is far more worthwhile than presents.

If it feels you are walking a path where your perception of your world is changing, you may feel that you are outside the mainstream world looking in. It may feel that you are watching some strange TV reality show where everyone is lost in the story, because in a sense many people are, but you are waking up!

As you wake up; as you question the illusions of your current outer reality, it will not be so easy in the beginning when events like Christmas, Valentine's Day and other major global illusionary events take place. It will not sit well with you, until you are more fully present. You will be able to see the bigger picture and put the puzzle pieces together of why the world is doing what it is doing, and you may even want to scream, *'STOP - this is not real'*, but you know you cannot, because it is none of your business. It is not your responsibility to change another's perceptions or their world. In fact it can be dangerous to enforce your beliefs on someone else before they are ready, causing a lot of chaos inside them and problems for you.

You will probably feel superior at these times, but also a sense of inferiority as the old you is still fighting to stay, wanting to belong by fitting in. As you see the masquerades of photos parading their way on Facebook, of the perfect family, the perfect relationship, the perfect Christmas, the perfect children, the perfect career... it may hurt inside. For even though you are beginning to realise it is all an illusion, and often what people reveal on the outside is not what is going on in their inner world, a part of you is not settled with this yet, a part of you wonders if what they show is real and if it is, then why is your life so lacking in comparison. There is unease in the beginning.

And all you can do is to surrender deeply.

As sadness, a feeling of loneliness arises, a feeling of not fitting in, a feeling of being an alien in a strange land, a feeling that the world has gone insane, instead of resisting this feeling, or trying to make yourself happy, or trying to be merry at Christmas, surrender to your feelings, surrender to them, for they are a gift. They are a part of the process of change taking place. It is not overly comfortable for the caterpillar to transform. The metamorphosis can be strange and uncomfortable, and when it's time to fly, there is a difficult transition to move the wings out of the cocoon and to let go and fly.

Imagine that the cycle where you have one foot in the old and one foot in the new is the cocoon stage of the butterfly. You were the caterpillar happily munching along, following the tribe, following the mass consciousness taking place, believing what you were told by the media, doing what you were told, trying to be happy when they said you should, trying to fit in, going along through addiction, over-eating, drug taking and drinking alcohol, sugar highs... munching away and being a caterpillar.

And then something happens, you notice something different and begin to become more present with your feelings, your inner world. Perhaps you start meditating and then you begin to question your outer reality and whether it is real. You then see that your perception of the world has changed; you are wanting to be that caterpillar again but you cannot; you also want to be the new you, the butterfly that understands all, that is able to fall into the flow of presence; that releases the suffering more easily; that is able to deeply let go and surrender graciously into the flow.

But you are not there yet. You have your wings but you also feel a sense of the caterpillar, of the old; you are in the soggy sticky place of the cocoon. All is dark, unknown, and scary, but you can't step backwards. You must allow your feelings to shift and change; you must allow your wings to fully form; you must let yourself feel those challenging emotions of anger, sadness and rage, for as you are able to do so, you are beginning to practice more and more loving kindness and compassion for self. And this loving kindness is what strengthens your wings ready for flight.

You cannot bypass this stage. It is part of the spiritual journey. The butterfly has always been a significant symbol for growth, change and transformation in life. As always, nature knows the way. Your life knows the way. Surrender deeply to the moment. Do not try to fight and be different from how you are today. It is all okay. There is no need to be happy at Christmas if you are not; no need to be something other than what you are. As you are, life accepts you; as you are, life loves you.

Chapter 27

~Stepping Out Into the Light~

Some of you are teachers. You teach not only by example but by your words, your actions, your writing and your creative expression. It can feel hard to begin to own your purpose, to own your reason for being on this planet. As the 'not good enough' voices rattle through your mind, it can be tough going in the beginning to believe you have anything worthy of sharing that can not only impact you as you share it, but also others who may be ready to hear the wisdom. You may cringe and not believe that you have wisdom that is ready to be shared and some may feel not only unworthy, but unsuitable teachers.

'You teach what you need to learn' is a well-known phrase in Western society, but nonetheless it is often true. So many of you feel you have nothing to offer or give to the world until you are fixed or have sorted out or healed certain aspects of your human personality, but it is in this moment that your own inner wisdom can come forth.

Many of you will have read books by someone who no longer has the issues or difficulties they write about. They have 'overcome' the challenges they are teaching about. Yet very few express what they know before they have dealt with it fully, for many are given the message that it is of no value what they know, if they are not able to practise it themselves. I am here to say that more people will hear someone speaking from current experience than from the past. If you share your light and your wisdom as you learn, and give yourself permission to share your story, not only will you heal as you share and find balance within, but people who are in the same position as you will more readily be able to hear what you have to say.

No need to continue hiding your light because you feel you are not whole yet. You are always whole; you are always where you need to be in the moment; you always have what you 'need' to know right now.

It can feel scary to share your inner guidance because you may feel on shaky ground with it all as you are still learning. You may feel that if you share and are not fully embodying the entire message, then you are a fake, but you are not. The deepest answers can come from your deepest pain.

If you can ask yourself questions and share the answers, you are gifting your light to others, not just yourself, and this is not fake. You are beyond the personality self and allowing your inner wisdom to shine a light on areas you too need assistance with.

All is well. All is in its proper place. Start from where you are.

It can feel scary to offer a difference of opinion or viewpoint when a group of people come together, but as you become more present, as you become more authentic, you will know that you must let your light shine regardless of what reaction or response you get from others.

As you share and the fear arises, you may get many different thoughts flooding your mind, thoughts such as:

"People are thinking – who does she think she is?"

"He is just a know-it-all!"

You may push buttons in those who think this, but you will also touch those who are ready to hear your unique wisdom, your own inner knowing. Some will be indifferent, some may hate you or your message, some may vacillate between dislike and like, but you are not responsible for how anyone responds to your intuitive awareness being shared. You are just being you, authentically you and are no longer hiding your light.

Shining your light does not mean forcing your views onto others or making people wrong. You can assertively and gently share what comes forth from within you. You came with a voice and that voice is to uplift, inspire and encourage others and yourself. And everyone has this same voice. People can hear what you say and discard it, or take it on board. It is entirely up to them. Take none of this personally. It is not personal.

Chapter 28

~Friendship and the Spiritual Path~

Some of you may find as you get older that forming friendships can seem a lot more challenging than when you were a child or in your school years. As your heart starts to open you may have this overwhelming yearning to really connect with others on a similar wavelength to you, but as you soon find out, opening your heart and meeting others who are opening their hearts, can feel like a long and lengthy journey.

In many ways you may spend long periods of time alone, or with people who are merely acquaintances that you know from work or have met in other places, with none of these people providing you with the heart-full intimacy you have been wanting since your heart began to open.

It is easy to become drawn to spiritual teachers, wanting friendship from those who teach you, or whom you relate to, more than the ordinary person on the street. One thing many of you do is to project what you want a friend to be, perhaps onto someone who will never be that way and so the friendships fizzle out and are short-lived. These friendships may last longer as you attempt to create something that is not there and never was, and some may end in an explosion of emotion.

The problem with becoming friends with a person who was once your spiritual teacher is that it is often hard to switch roles from teacher to friend, more so for the teacher. You may begin to realise you do not want to be taught by this person, you simply want to chat and be friends, but the relationship was based on a more serious connection of support and help offered.

Your spirit is yearning for laughter, fun and freeing conversations, with activities that light you up inside, but with the opportunity for deep and meaningful chats when a good friend is needed.

If your last friendship ended in a challenging way, and perhaps you have a pattern of difficult friendships with your own sex, it can feel hard to trust others after this, but you must trust, trust that as you awaken and become aware of what your real needs are, you will attract those types of people into your world, people who want to walk side-by-side with you and not teachers wanting to impart their wisdom to you.

Becoming more present enables you to be in the right place at the right time to meet someone who may be on a similar wavelength and is also equally craving fun times, not being deeply spiritual all the time.

The people you need to meet will arrive in your life at the perfect time, not a moment before. In the meantime the most important friendship you can develop is with you. Find light-hearted things to do with your day, paint, draw, photograph the world around you, listen to music, dance, or take yourself out for coffee or lunch. Don't miss out on things people normally do together. Do them alone, and in this way you value your time, your space, and your place in the world.

Loneliness

For those of you who are experiencing loneliness, you will find that over time, spending time with yourself is a blessing not a curse; you will find moments of value in the simplest of things. Going for a walk becomes a sojourn; a coffee on your own in a café becomes a quiet reflective retreat time where you are among the living, but at ease within your own company.

The greatest friendship is always with self, for in another you are meeting yourself anyway. What better place to begin a new friendship than with you first?

Once you are fully at ease in your own company, embracing any flaws or character quirks that may have caused you deep suffering in the past, when you meet others on your path, they will meet you in total acceptance because they feel the ease with which you are living.

As you accept the person you are, others will accept you. Until this moment you will still have people in your world who will judge you and criticize you, for you are judging and criticising you, and as you accept and nurture who you are, with greater loving kindness, your world opens up. People will come to you who want to sit in the radiance of your open heart. This is how real friendship begins – from within.

If you experience intense loneliness, it is perhaps time to make peace with this pain.

Recall the feelings, allow them to wash through you as a storm washes through a forest; stay strong in your present moment awareness, but allow the cleansing quality of simply 'being' to heal and prepare you for new beginnings.

Find your own value; your own self-respect; your own beauty. See the anger, rage, fear, sadness and anxiety as a friend, not an enemy. Only then can you release the cloak of loneliness, the cloak of invisibility. Only then can you become visible by seeing the suffering as it is, as unloved and under-nourished qualities within you. And as you do so, the cloak is shed, you are invisible no more, for the world mirrors the new you.

How to Keep the Heart Open

A challenge for many of you is staying open when your pattern is that you close for protection. When you feel fear within, you may instantly find a way to ignore the feeling. You get active, shut down, eat comfort foods, have sex, watch TV, surf the net. For anyone who has experienced anxiety and panic attacks, fear can feel like the greatest enemy and you will do anything you can to not feel it, yet your pushing it away merely brings it back stronger and bigger than you experienced before. Keeping the heart open during fear gives you room and space to make friends with you.

You will quite naturally want to avoid any difficult emotion. It is like running away from a tiger or a bear. The fear is that predator, and you will do all you can to avoid harm or death. If you have ever had a dream where you have been chased by a lion or other predator, you may have woken up in a sweat of panic, but if you had lingered in the dream and allowed the lion to devour you, or you merged with the lion, you would discover the gift in surrendering to the fear. Surrendering is empowering; it is not disempowering; it is not about giving up in life; it is about giving your all for life.

Allow yourself to give 'you' the care and attention you need, instead of distance and detachment from who you really are.

If another person says or does something that makes you feel very angry or upset, you can go into the old pattern of fighting against your feelings and then go back into blame and resentment, or you can try a new way, stopping in that moment, feeling those feelings and becoming the watcher instead.

Don't try to be present with your emotions and feelings in order to change them.

Being present allows them to simply be and sends a signal, that as you are, you are worthy of acceptance and care. The emotions over time dissolve on their own, without force or will, or you will be guided to practice forgiveness or to get professional help. Again all of this will take place naturally.

Sacred Solitude

Some of you may experience a deep sense of solitude on your life path, and for some time intense feelings of loneliness may flood you. You may not understand why you find it hard to keep friendships or make new friends. You may be a perfectly nice person but seem to be alone most of the time. Consider this a blessing – not a curse.

Imagine that you came into this lifetime brimming with enthusiasm, full of vibrancy, joy, socially confident, a social butterfly and for your whole life you are surrounded by people. You love being around people. They give you a feeling of belonging, but being alone...no, this is not for you. It's too noisy inside, nothing to distract you from what is going on emotionally for you, so you spent most of your life with others and for the most part you were essentially happy.

Now what if those of you who are not experiencing this were actually choosing this solitude? Perhaps in other lifetimes you have experienced countless social whirlwind experiences, and while they were happy, as happy as you could be, relying on outward appearances, this time you decided your soul wants to experience a deeper connection, a deeper wisdom, a deeper joy, a deeper love.

This is where you are a willing participant in 'sacred solitude'.

It is no coincidence that you are on your spiritual path seemingly alone. You, as a soul, decided to challenge yourself to find that sense of belonging, that sense of support, from within this time. And it may seem a far more challenging life than surrounding yourself with people and living that happy-chappy life mentioned above, but your soul wants to grow and evolve and so you chose the path of solitude.

Little did you know it would feel so lonely, but over time as you begin to realise the importance of enjoying your own company, becoming present with 'what is', truly allowing your feelings to be felt and accepted, you begin to feel a new experience, an awakening!

Your heart begins to open, and love begins to pour out of you and be felt. But not love in the human way, which is limited.

Human love has an 'on/off' switch and is based on attraction or attachment. Divine love is limitless, shines on everything like the sun. There is no 'off' switch and this is what you have come to experience if you chose the path of solitude.

A path of solitude needn't last forever, and it generally does not, but your life will appear lacking in the human factor until you have awakened to what you came here to experience, a remembrance of who you really are, or an experience of divine love that enables you to experience the world completely differently and unconditionally.

When you begin to see that your aloneness has a purpose too, you will see that you are not really alone, you never were. To discover that there is a reason why friends have come and gone and why you keep experiencing a lack of people in your life, you will become more focused inwardly.

This is the way of the wise.

You came here to love.

Not to be loved.

Just to love.

When you love from your whole being, you do not feel the desire or yearning to be loved back. Because you are not 'doing' love, you are 'being' love and this feels an entirely different experience from human egoic love.

This love radiates from your heart centre; it is a warm, soft opening. You love the trees and concrete on the ground in the same way that you love your dog or your partner. You love as your dog does, unconditionally. Even if a dog is mistreated it keeps coming back to love, for this is all it knows, to love. That is its inherent being.

So your sacred alone time can be sublime.

Are you beginning to see that all has a purpose? That nothing is wrong and no-one has been dealt a bad deck of cards? You always had these resources within you and you always had support around you. It may not be in the form of human physical support but universal support, spiritual support, love support. You are never alone.

Chapter 29

~Feeling the Flaws Opening the Doors~

To be honest, being human is not easy. You come into this world full of clarity, openness, awareness and then go through the journey of self-awareness through interactions with others. This can be a great influence if you are surrounded by well-balanced individuals, but this is rarely the case, and because of this most people are retrained out of the openness, awareness, self-acceptance and confidence from an early age.

The more present you become on your life path, the more some aspects of your personality and the choices you make will bother you. Before, they were hidden by all of the human distractions in the world, but now they are not only playing a game of peek-a-boo with you, but many of them are screaming at you for care and attention. You cannot run away from what you may call flaws. They are part of the awakening process. Some call it the dark side, the shadow self, but these flaws are your doorway through to the change and peace you may have been longing for within your heart and soul.

Your flaws can come to the surface in an overly loud and theatrical style. Initially you become really resistant to them. They cause the story of 'not good enough' to play on repeat for a while, until you realise that for anything to change, these flaws need to be seen and accepted first.

If you are in denial of your flaws or quirks, they cannot change. In the beginning, it is easy when the light of the present moment shines on the flaws so strongly, to go through the old process of beating yourself up for being a certain way. Your awareness of your flaws can turn into name calling, telling yourself you are mean, unpleasant, controlling etc...

So you may spend some time criticising who you are, wanting so much for this not to be so. Once you are aware of your flaws you often want them gone in super quick time. But they do not need beating into submission, they need to be accepted. Yes, you may have traits of wanting to be right, thinking people are wrong, demanding people to accept what you say, but in turn not offering others the same right to their beliefs and opinions, and this in itself can be extremely hard to accept.

However, until you are able to genuinely accept and own these flaws, the same patterns will continue. When you are ready to accept them, your heart will open more and you will find a greater sense of peace within. You are not a horrible person for acting or being a certain way towards others; you are aware and this is a huge step.

Every human has flaws they would rather not have. You are not alone in the suffering you feel. Because of these character traits you may feel powerless to change. You are not powerless. Your awareness and acknowledgement of them is where you power lies. From herein you can experience an awakening of your personal worth, value and self-confidence.

Chapter 30

~Poop or Get Off The Pot~

A great astrologer online posted a run-down of what the Sun sign Aries needed to do regarding a new moon in the year 2014. Neil D. Paris said:

"This is it. Make or Break. Poop or get off the pot. My recommendation: keep going and when you're ready to quit or bail, go the extra mile and then decide."

Many teachers out there often say don't give up when you are so close, or keep going, it's just around the corner, give up now and you will miss out. It is easy to take this as a carrot dangling on the string, always chasing the future dream, the castles in the sky that never happen. But there comes a point in life when it is time to follow through, to keep going, and even if you feel like quitting whatever you are doing creatively, to keep going through the *'I may as well quit, this is obviously not working'* phase.

Of course as was mentioned earlier, sometimes it is important to quit, to 'fail', to make mistakes. That part of frustration involves slowing you down so you do not miss the junction where you need to get off. And then you get to do something which feels quite natural to you and you are nearing the end of it, and you suddenly doubt yourself and your abilities. You look at your creation and think it is not good enough (yet again!) and think it's time to throw in the towel. Yet you know that this time it's different.

In the past you felt you could throw in the towel and start something new again, because it was not your time for that creation to materialise; it was not part of your life journey. But this time is different. You know you cannot get off the pot - it is time to poop as Neil so eloquently put it (smile).

If you get to the point where you look at your creation and you cannot think what else you could do and another idea has not sprung forward to put your heart into - this creation is it.

Your creative juices need the follow through on this project. You may not know why, you may not know if it is going to be a success, but for your own self-esteem and self-worth you need to complete it. You need to finish it and to be able to look back and say to yourself *'I did it!'* *'I finished the painting'*, *'I put my all into the business'*, *'I finished the book'*...the list goes on.

But you did it, you completed it. The next part of the journey is in the lap of the gods. The universe knows the way, always did and always will. A time for trust is called for, immense trust and faith that what you have created is important, is part of your journey; otherwise something else would have come to take its place.

If you have not felt distracted, if you have felt focused, if you have felt committed, this is it!

Seize the opportunity to expand your view of both yourself and the possibilities in your life. Your potential is far greater than you ever imagined it could be. Even when you tried to control your life, perhaps through creating your reality, the ideas you had and the dreams you had were tiny in comparison to the real depth and meaning that comes from allowing your life to unfold, and trusting the signals for change and creation.

Anything is possible, but in the sense that if it is for your highest good, it is yours.

Anything else will be stepping stones on the path to change, and when you are ready you will go full steam ahead, not a moment before. No force necessary, no need to steer the river or control the tide of your life. Life knows the way, always has, always does. Trust this.

Trust your innate ability to forge new arenas in your creativity, new arenas in what is possible. Follow through as your heart flowers and expands; follow through as your instincts begin to shine out. You were blessed when you came into this lifetime and that never changed, it just appeared that it did.

You were not abandoned by life, or given a bad deck of cards; you were given the life that would allow the greatest possible potential for growth and love. If your heart has felt weary from setbacks, heartache and failure, take heed, it was all necessary.

If you want others to see you, the real you needs to shine through. And if you can allow your unique talents and energies to flow through what you do, you will be seen. The people who need your abilities will find you and discover you and have their own journeys triggered and supported as you shine your light. It is a process of discovery. Discovering what it is you are here to be, do and give.

Love is the supreme journey most of you came here to express into the world. If your dreams and inspirations do not contain love, but a need to please and look good, you are not on your life path. Your heart needs nothing more than to give love and this is what you are here to experience.

Chapter 31

~What Are You Here To Give?~

New growth comes when you least expect it, sometimes even in the middle of winter a new leaf emerges from the branch of a tree or bush. You sit and you wonder how will it survive the winter when the frost comes? But it has taken the risk to bud when it was ready. You may be in the winter of your life right now, thinking there is nothing growing, nothing new emerging from you, when a sudden surge of growth happens in the middle of your winter life cycle. You are no different from the trees or bushes, growth can and does come at any time.

The tree may not burst forth with many leaves and blossoms until the spring, but this does not mean that small and seemingly insignificant changes aren't taking place now, and often these small changes lead to bigger changes later on.

Honour your commitment to change; honour your commitment to accepting who you are in this present moment; honour your focus, your awareness, and your understanding coming forth now. This is all good and all part of the process of the evolving universe.

Large bumble bees are sometimes out until winter, and it is surprising to see bees out so late, yet they are little miracles, determined to find nourishment and nectar for the queen, long after all the other types of bees have gone into the next life. This is how focused you are right now; otherwise you would not be reading this book.

Something inside you wanted confirmation, wanted confirmation that you were doing okay, that you are not a bad person if you do not have it all together, or know where you are going in life. Something inside you wanted this message and brought you to it, a reminder from your inner self that you are exactly where you need to be right now in your life cycle.

Your winter may feel as if it has lasted a very long time, but if you look to see where you are now; not materially; not relationship-wise; not career-wise, but who you are inside; if you are becoming aware of the bigger picture in your life; if you are more aware of what is right for you and what is not, then you have made great strides and progress. You have your buds growing on that tree. It may not be full of leaves, but every beginning must start somewhere.

Even if life does not feel like anything is happening, it is. You are like nature, in the winter of your life, where new growth takes place, sometimes on the surface, but often deep beneath in your root system. You integrate what you have learned. Remember this when you doubt where you are in your life.

Nature never doubts; nature just is. There is immense beauty and growth always taking place, even in those harsh winters when everything feels cold, bare and devoid of life, life is always flowing through everything and within every one of you.

Chapter 32

~Begin to Take Yourself Seriously~

Becoming focused, clearing through the debris of old baggage that you have been carrying most of your life, you will come to a time when something inside you shifts. This is a natural process, one where you need to walk through the storm of feelings, to feel your emotions, feel your pain, feel your suffering and then forgive your suffering, forgive those who have hardened your heart and then you begin to see potential in your life, real potential.

Real potential, soul potential, is different from ego potential. Ego potential has ideas of what it thinks you should be doing, perhaps to prove yourself to others, or perhaps to get you out of an undesirable set of circumstances. No, real potential is a glimmer of everything coming together.

If you set up a business, people will come to your website, and any challenges or difficulties that you may feel are going to be hard, suddenly, people are there to show you how to move through them, or the money you need arrives, or the inspiration to follow through, comes. Your focus is deepening and your self-belief is growing. This all came from acceptance of what is, from facing those demons most people run away from and try to distract themselves from.

There is no way around the pain. You need to walk through it, for this is where your potential lies. The suffering was masking your true potential, your real reason for being here. When you masked or hid from your pain through avoidance strategies, your dreams, your goals and desires took on an energy of 'doing something that appears amazing or good to the outside world'.

Perhaps you had this strong desire to travel the world and be a writer, writing yourself around the world, and this notion was romanticised by the movies you watched. You wanted an easy life, just writing, being rich and enjoying that lifestyle, yet as nothing came to you to assist in this dream, you were left in a mountain of despair and feelings of failure again.

Like the phoenix you came from those ashes of lost dreams, those ashes containing the real diamond of your life, your soul purpose.

Your purpose often contains a gift that you can share with the world. It not only feels good to you, but it gives something to the planet in some way. Perhaps you make a product that makes life easier for someone, or you create beautiful photography that inspires someone to visit far off lands, or you speak about your experiences in life and it uplifts and empowers people; the list is endless, there is no wrong life purpose.

Your real life purpose comes from love, and in essence your purpose is simply to live, and through that living come divine attributes and skills that you brought into this lifetime. You chose this lifetime; you chose your challenges at a soul level, even those incredibly painful ones that the mind judges as impossible to have been chosen.

Begin to Take Yourself Seriously

The universe that creates worlds is experiencing through you. This includes all the pain, fear, anger, rage and onto the joy, peace and grace you experience. And there comes a time when you take full responsibility for your gifts and talents, and you make the choice to put your all into them. Your heart is guiding you and life is supporting you. This is when you have hit the jackpot; this is when you are in the stream of energy that was there for you as and when the time became right. And this is often far more empowering than your human personality dreamed up for you in this lifetime.

Always ask if what you are doing is for the love of doing it, or for need to do it for others? Is it a natural thing to you, like riding a bike or walking?

And then you take it seriously. You are ready to be who you really are and it took walking the valleys and hills of life, struggling through the storms and thunder and lightning, having the earth move beneath your feet, to come to here.

Chapter 33

~Self Esteem and Purpose~

Before your purpose and understanding of why you are here unfolds, if you have led a life with the story of 'not good enough', you will have discovered that rage, fear, envy and resentment may plague your days. Yet as you will have experienced, once you begin to become more present with these feelings, they pass through you more quickly and as you start to express your unique talents and abilities in small ways, your desire to forgive and let go of your judgments will increase. Holding onto the old way of viewing your world will change.

It is not simply a case of you must let go of rage or you must let go of anger or your life will create more reasons to be angry. I know this is the popular belief among empowerment and spiritual circles now, but you go through a process of release, and being told that you create experiences based on your rage, your fear, your resentment, simply breeds feelings of guilt and further self-flagellation, when there is no need.

Your time will come when you have no need for these emotions nearly so much, but it's not a fast food way of change; it is a gradual process and a willingness to change. But even the willingness to change only takes place as and when you are ready. No force, no pushing through or fighting against with positive affirmations, but with gentleness and openness. And if now you feel change will not come and never will, know that it will, maybe not straight away, granted, but it will come. It's impossible for it to remain the same; it's the way of the universe, the way of life and of nature.

One day something will shift. For example you may have a neighbour who is extremely noisy, who plays their radio at high volume, but you are powerless to stop this happening. For years you may have banged on the wall or ceiling; for years you may have cussed and wished them unpleasant things (Yes, you all do this unless you are saints of course), and this caused you to feel extremely stressed.

Then one day, after several months of paying attention to your surroundings, meditating more, finding more reasons to simply 'be' instead of 'doing' all the time, the noise starts again and you are aware that the anger and rage and blame are there still, but instead of simply screaming, you decide you want to see this person differently.

Perhaps you begin to see that they are not deliberately doing this to piss you off, and you begin to see that they are suffering too and do not know how to live without constant noise in their lives. You may begin to see differently. Perhaps you do not have compassion yet, but you have awareness, and this is the beginning. Awareness means something is shifting. This is not an overnight process, but it means something is happening now, something different.

And as things shift, you begin to see those people who pushed your buttons in a different light. You see them as different, unique, and doing what is right for them on their path and that you walk different paths even though they may look similar. You see the mirrors in your reactions and want to see people differently, instead of wanting to see them in a bad light. This is progress; this is change, even if it seems small. This is how everything begins.

With every small way you express your purpose, from the simple writing of a poem, to the painting of a picture, your confidence will grow and your self-esteem will slowly blossom.

Allowing your life to unfold naturally, instead of trying to force through to success, you build a very strong foundation beneath the house of your inner self. You build a strong foundation from which your creation can flourish – a safe home where the new can begin.

It all begins with a strong foundation or root system, and patience is necessary. Patience is not a cuss word (even though it may feel that way from time-to-time), but patience is the way you grow your roots; it is a way that when your creation comes out into the light of day for others to see and experience, it is solid, real and will not be knocked over.

So praise the day that rage came into your life; praise the day anger and resentment showed themselves to you; praise how your new awareness is awakening you to who you really are.

These are not emotions to be slated or dismissed or forced to change. You cannot do any of that until you are ready. Question any teacher who promises you instant healing or success, trust your gut instincts and follow your own natural flow in life. This is all you can do, for it is your path to walk on and your journey to take.

Doorways of Potential

There Are Many Paths and Many Doorways on Your Soul Journey.

Don't miss the doors opening because of tunnel vision.

On the human journey it is so easy to get lost in the mirage of desire and wanting. Unless you have released and brought into balance what is taking place within, you tend to make choices that are inflexible and set goals that are so definite and so precise. While this is all a part of growing as a person and evolving your spirit, you come to a stage where it is time to take stock.

Imagine walking down a corridor and at the end of the corridor is this bright flashing light. This light is what you want and desire. Perhaps you want to be a dancer, or want a new car or house in a certain area, so you power walk down that corridor and attempt to open the door, but even though the light is flashing brightly you cannot turn the handle and when you try to force it open you meet intense resistance.

That door was not meant for you, but because of your conditioning, your patterns, your ego thinking that you ought to be doing this specific thing, you are so determined to have this thing you want, be it through goal setting or attempts at creating your reality, you forget to ask if this is really what you need.

What is so important on your journey through life when making choices is to ask:

'Do I need this?'

'Why do I really want this?'

'Is there anything beneath this want that may be messing with my judgments here?'

More often than not, if you keep meeting resistance, this door is not for you. This does not mean something similar is not for you, but you could be missing out on the doorways along that corridor through fixed goals and desires.

The next time you are heading for a door, remember to ask the above questions, and if you are not sure, keep very open, open to being still, until the answers or directions come. Be open to a potentially completely different doorway. It is best not to try to limit the universe, for the universe is limitless, any number of doorways can be available to you.

Sometimes you may find that the thing you fear the most in life, which may also excite you, is related to your life purpose. That fear is your doorway; that fear may leave you cowering beneath your own potential. So do not discount those fears and phobias; they could be signalling you for a bigger change than you could ever have imagined as you power walked down that corridor of life. Be wary of loud flashing signs seeming to be impressive and important. Go with the heart's guidance and listen to life's signals - life always knows the way - trust it.

Chapter 34

~The Best Laid Plans~

Sometimes 'the best laid plans of mice and men' do not work out the way you want them to. It is easy to forge ahead into a new project full of enthusiasm, listing out what you want to happen, in what order, and how, but life does not work that way.

If you have a mild winter the trees will blossom early, but if there is a sudden frost the blossoms may die, but the difference between nature and humanity is generally that humans will try to force the blossoms back into their buds, willing them back into safety. Winter may come any minute and the blossoms will shrivel and die.

Nature knows differently.

If nature has a mild winter, it adapts to the changes. Not being fixated on one direction, it simply adjusts from within. To nature it works together, following the rays of the sun, the water it consumes and insects may come out earlier than anticipated by humans, but to nature it's just being nature. It does not look at timescales or clocks, or whether it should or should not blossom and grow. It just goes with the flow of life and does what it does. Completely flexible and no fear of whether winter will suddenly rush in or that its blossoms will die.

Nature is completely in the moment. Life and death are one and the same. No judgment about which is better or worse, it just is. Are you able to do the same with any creative projects you are involved in?

Perhaps you started something in the Autumn and said to yourself that Spring would be a good time to have everything completed by, and you write, or you paint, or create in some other way, but instead of feeling inspired you reach a wall of nowhere else to go. Are you finished now? How can you know if it is time to finish and let the world see your creation?

When it is time, you will know.

Don't give up when you feel you've hit a wall. Sometimes this does not mean the end at all. Instead allow grace to fill you, take a break and meditate. Trust your guidance from within.

Chapter 35

~Money, Money, Money~

Money is something many people have difficulty receiving or relating to. The saying *'Money makes the world go around'* is essentially true, but in the sense that money is energy and if you replace it with the word love, love makes the world go around. However, not many are able to see money as love because of unpleasant memories, patterns and conditioned thinking related to money.

Many teachers have written about this topic. The saying *'Money is the root of all evil'*, has been passed down through generations and generations of families and people, and this has had a big effect on humanity's view of money. If you have not had a positive experience of money in your life, it is probably one of the most challenging areas to resolve and to gain a greater understanding of what is taking place.

Some teachers will say that all you need to do to have more money in your life is to affirm that you are rich and wealthy, or that money loves you etc... But most of these teachers do not have such heavily loaded programs that many people do today. Allowing money into your life is not as easy as 1, 2, 3 Abracadabra! It can take time.

Time is the journey, the journey through first embracing your experiences of money, second, your feelings around having or not having money, and third, a way to forgive your relationship with money. Money often has so many hidden agendas and beliefs. Most people feel the only way to have money is to work hard, often doing something they do not enjoy. Some believe that money is easy to receive, but not to keep. And some believe that money is unspiritual so that if they have money they get rid of it super-fast so they can be spiritual human beings.

Of course, all these beliefs are false, illusions built on a history of illusions upon illusions. Many cultures frown upon ease, grace and receiving wealth the easy way. If someone found it easy to become wealthy, some people will say, *'It's alright for some'* or *'Oh, how the other half live!'* And in doing so, they are saying it is not alright for them.

As hard as it may feel to hear, sometimes having little or no money is part of your divine plan. Your soul may have chosen a life of seemingly outer poverty to experience what really matters, to find a way of seeing the sublime and beautiful in the simplicity of life. It can also be a big challenge to trust that life will take care of you every step of the way.

Money comes when you are ready.

Money does not come if you are not ready.

If it is in your life, it is meant to be in your life.

If it is not, you are not meant to have it in your life.

This will not change until you are ready once again.

Oh, I know how mean this may sound. It would be so easy if you just said, *'I am a money magnet, money flows to me easily and effortlessly'* and TA DA! There it is. And yes, this may happen for some, but only if it's part of their divine plan. For many this is not the case. It takes a journey through your beliefs about money, a journey of self-compassion, awakening the heart, making friends with the pain and suffering, and eventually a trickle of belief within you will change. One day you may wake up and genuinely feel (not faking it) *'Hey, I am ready. Hey, I actually do deserve to have more money.'* And then money will flow into your world.

You receive exactly what you are ready to receive.

In the beginning you may only be ready to receive smaller sums, because there has been a lot of fear around the topic of money. Some people connect money and death as a belief. A family member may have died through stress about money worries, and so their children take on the belief that money equals the people they love hurting or dying. This is why sometimes it comes in, at first, in trickles, and as they begin to expand their awareness, open their hearts through self-compassion and loving kindness, they feel ready to receive more.

This all happens in good time, in perfect timing, and not a moment before.

Ask yourself now, deep down, are you ready for money?

If you say to yourself, *'I am a magnet for money. Money comes to me easily and effortlessly!'* Do you believe it? And more importantly do you feel it?

If you do not feel it, it is time to surrender and welcome the feelings in. And from there you can begin to question your beliefs about money, and dig a little deeper to see where they may need to change.

This change will come, as and when it's time, not a moment before.

Try not to force the issue. You are not in control of this. Life will bring you the answers you need; life will bring you what you need to know, and life will show you what you are here to learn and why a feeling of lack may be in your world at this time. But most of all, do not beat yourself up if money is not there, and do not try to force money to come to you through positive thinking. Words are not enough, you need to feel what you think and say. If you do not, it is not time. You have other things to be doing and experiencing. You have other things yet to unfold.

Divine Timing!

I know it sucks sometimes, but this is life. Everything takes place in its own perfect time and this goes for you and your life too.

Surrender to 'what is'.

Chapter 36

~Potential~

"And the day came when the risk to remain tight in a bud was more painful than the risk it took to blossom"

~Anaïs Nin

It is so easy to judge others as being slow to recognise when they need to make change, or to judge people who moan and complain about their jobs, relationships, business etc... But often people need to reach a tipping point before they choose to make a change and be ready for something new in their lives.

Some people consciously choose to remain the same. It is possible that a part of their life story was for Consciousness to experience drama and challenge. This sounds a really challenging life path to have pre-chosen, but as Consciousness does not define anything as bad, good or otherwise, it is simply another role being played. A tree plays the role of tree; a dog plays the role of Consciousness as dog; a person fights against life, the government or anything is Consciousness experiencing fighting.

There is no separation existing between the role and the experience, the human and the story. Consciousness is expansive and unlimited, and if you were to live a life full of drama and were going to experience that all your life, you would not have this book in your hands; you would not be questioning your reality, or the world around you and within you.

People who are primarily asleep, stay asleep. They would not feel lacking or yearning for a more empowered life; they would be unconsciously content with the drama of their life journey, for this would be Consciousness deliberately experiencing that story. You chose differently. Your unique essence may have already experienced a drama-full life.

If you know someone who is depressed most of the time, and you bring to them your wisdom and insights, and they do not hear you, you may get frustrated with them, but it's not your job to fix them or make them be something other than what they are. If and when they are ready for change it will happen. The right teacher, person, opportunity will come their way and more than likely it won't be you.

You may even have to accept that they may have chosen on a soul level to experience this life for a reason. Perhaps it is tolerance you need to learn, or perhaps total acceptance of who they are right now; perhaps learning to love unconditionally. You may even find that if you were totally accepting and just loved them, without offering them any suggestions, they might be influenced by your example of living a more empowered life.

The next time you watch or hear a friend repeating the same story about something they are struggling with, remember that they may actually be processing it on a deeper level each time. The more challenging it becomes for them, the closer they are to making a change. As in life, sometimes it needs to become chaotic before people stand up to be counted. This happens individually too.

Slow Progress

If you are in the midst of embracing your world, your feelings, allowing yourself to hear and sense your intuition, perhaps the next step for you is no step and you are being ushered and guided to simply 'be', but you are faced with a friend or co-worker who is a huge over-achiever. This can be a struggle for the ego, not the inner self, but the small self that still longs for control.

If someone lives in the flow, following opportunities and inner guidance as and when they naturally unfold, this is passion and living from the heart.

If someone counts the rate of their success based on how many tasks they complete in one day, this is not passion, it's over-achieving.

Over-achievers eventually get burned out later in life, for they live their lives in the goal-driven mindset, which is not something that is sustainable. The energy of the human body cannot live with a 'go, go, go' attitude all the time without burning out. Simply 'being' is heavily resisted by over-achievers. The thought of simply 'being' would feel like a pointless waste of precious 'doing' time.

But if you have over-achievers among your family or friends when you are just beginning to feel the experience of simply being, it can be hard for the ego not to feel wobbly and frail when it plays its usual comparison game.

You may have gotten out of bed, meditated, had a lovely walk, done some writing or photography and your over-achieving friend has finished 5 projects, cooked tonight's dinner, baked a cake and submitted a proposal, and all before lunchtime. This can make your fragile ego feel like a failure for not being like them, feeling that you are not getting anything done.

You may even feel that this person is flying ahead of you and will beat you across the finishing line of life. But it's not a competition, it's not a race. Life is a journey and you are the journey.

Let the over-achievers be. They may or may not come to realise that their way of operating is not healthy or helpful for their own life path in the long term. What is important for you is to listen to your inner voice and inner guide. Whatever an over-achiever gains in one day you may gain a far more rooted experience in the now, and your 'doing' may be easier as it is coming from grace, not effort or wilful force.

This is not to say the over-achiever will not experience outward success, but it may mean that your success may feel more valuable to you, because you are not chasing the next future goal where you think happiness may be. You are not chasing anything, but embracing the joy, the beauty, the grace and happiness that can only be found in the present moment of NOW.

This world needs a good mix of people. Over-achievers, perfectionists, performers, meditators... the list goes on. If nature had only one type of tree, the world would simply not be the same, would it? Bless every path for all paths are equally valid.

What you see as over-achieving and too much 'doing' may to the over-achiever be exciting, thrilling and thriving in life. They may also envy your more laid-back approach. It is part of the human condition, comparison games. None are better or worse, just different.

Chapter 37

~Fear of Being Seen~

As was mentioned a little while ago, an artist who feels visible and who feels valuable and worthwhile will be seen more than perhaps a more seasoned artist who is hiding behind a wall of fear.

There comes a time on your life path when it is your time to be seen. You may have been holding back for some time, developing your project or creation, and perhaps poking your head out a little, and more people are valuing your work, but you have not quite moved out of your comfort zone. Perhaps you place your artwork on the web, but are feeling guided to submit it for a gallery showing.

You may be feeling this reluctant fear; a fear that if real people see your art in person, you will get to see and hear what people outside your comfort zone really feel about your creation, your baby. On your site it was safe because you were in control. You controlled what was shown, who was invited, and if you received any bad comments you could respond or block the person, but at a physical gallery you do not have this choice. You are revealing yourself in all your colours.

It feels safe in the comfort zone. You probably have friends and family who admire and say they like your work, but strangers outside may not say such nice things. They have no need to be as pleasant towards you, but can you risk remaining tightly inside your safe space when a whole world out there is ready to see you, all of who you are?

There is a well-known saying:

"Our deepest fear is not that we are inadequate. Our deepest fear is that we are powerful beyond measure. It is our light, not our darkness that most frightens us. We ask ourselves, Who am I to be brilliant, gorgeous, talented, fabulous? Actually, who are you not to be? You are a child of God. Your playing small does not serve the world. There is nothing enlightened about shrinking so that other people won't feel insecure around you. We are all meant to shine, as children do. We were born to make manifest the glory of God that is within us. It's not just in some of us; it's in everyone. And as we let our own light shine, we unconsciously give other people permission to do the same. As we are liberated from our own fear, our presence automatically liberates others."

From 'A Return To Love' by *Marianne Williamson*

This is what you fear. Not that you might fail, or that people may not like what you say or do, but that people may actually love what you do! You fear success and fear discovering that you are actually far more brilliant, talented and beautiful than you ever thought possible. You are scared of your brilliance. The light within you dazzles you so much that you cannot believe it is actually you.

Indeed, who are you not to let your light shine? This world is not here so that you can shrink and hide forever. There was a safety and purpose in your shrinking before. You needed to come together fully inside so that when you pushed up through the earth your buds and stem were strong enough to withstand the elements, and so that your light could shine. Like a rose blossoming for the first time, your scent is ready to blow through this world with an almighty rapture and joy. Do not hold back anymore. The world is now ready for you, and you are ready. Embrace your fear, feel it, let it come up and be held in your present moment awareness. Remove the cloak of invisibility and let your radiant light be shone.

There is no turning back now.

The rock has vanished.

There is nowhere else to go or hide.

The world needs you now. Do not hide anymore.

It is time to take to the stage and join in the dance of life.

Chapter 38

~Preparing For Change~

Change is not always as easy as a walk in the park. It often comes with hidden emotions that rise up to the surface. Sometimes your current reality may need to change. Whom you share a home with, what you envisioned in your relationships, perhaps you need to move house, let go of friends who are weighing you down, take a new career path completely alien to you. All of this can be incredibly scary to the ego.

The ego likes the known, the familiar. Even if the familiar is painful, it is still known. The unknown, even if it could be joyful, uplifting and inspiring is still unknown to the ego, so it will often drag up experiences from the past to cause suffering or to intensify the fear.

All the 'what ifs' will come out of the proverbial woodwork of your mind.

If the change means at some point a loved one you are incredibly close to will no longer be a regular part of your life, the struggle between flowering and shining, and staying the same and hiding, can still be taking place inside. Welcome these feelings. Take a deep breath and welcome them in.

Breathe in the fear of change; breathe in the fear of loss or the fear of failure.

Your mind will do anything to remain safe, well as safe as a mind could ever feel.

You could have been in a job for many, many years, fulfilling the same role for what seemed like a decade, a role that is familiar, but is becoming increasingly stressful and challenging each day. The thought of completely changing the role is frightening, but the thought of staying where you are is equally, if not more, frightening. It is this tipping point that causes you to allow the change to take place. Sometimes all it takes is a swing towards the feeling of something new to see how much the old no longer serves a purpose in your world.

You could be in a long term relationship, one where you deeply love the person, but you have become more like brother and sister. You do not feel like partners anymore, and what you want differs so much from what he or she wants now. But your heart tugs for the familiar. The thought of letting go of someone who loves and accepts you exactly as you are scares the bejabers out of you. For your ego is telling you, you will never meet anyone like him or her again.

The ego will do this. This is part and parcel of any change. It will fight tooth and nail to keep you in its own safe comfort zone (or discomfort zone). It will even have you question your relationship or your job, looking to see if you can make it work, to see if you can get new gems out of old dirt. But as you have been trying this for years and you were not able to make something magical that had lost its magic, you need to keep focused on the now. Allow yourself to believe that your life is unfolding and it is releasing what is no longer for you anymore. You will not be left starving by the edge of the roadside be it physically starving or emotionally. You are so much more resourceful than you believe you are.

Change, after a long time of things remaining the same, can feel like giving birth. You may feel anxious, you may feel teary, but you will know it is now time. There will be a mixture of emotions from sadness about things not working the way you had hoped, and tears of knowing that your time has come and you have been inside that box for too long, and you are being signalled it is time to leave the box of the known; it is time to be seen. Your heart will help you realise this. As it opens, you will feel a knowing no matter how hard the mind tries to have you think otherwise.

In the moment you flow; in the moment you breathe; in the moment you believe – yes, now is the time for change, there is no turning back. There is no remaining the same; no holding your talents inside. It is time to reveal who you are.

Reveal who you are and what you have to give to this world. Far more than your small self ever had you believe. You can do this. Trust that you have within you what you need. You are not alone, you never were, and you always had helpers and support by your side. Non-physical family nurturing you, stroking your back when you felt unsupported by outer life, touching your heart when it felt crushed by what no longer worked. Encouraging you, inspiring you with ideas, untethering you from the beliefs you had held onto for so long about who you thought you were.

And now it is time to come home to you.

Step out onto that shifting carpet and know you are strong enough to ride the waves of change.

You deserve joy.

You deserve abundance.

You deserve freedom and grace.

And the time is NOW.

Break through the illusions of your past, of your old withered thinking, the patterns that kept you safe, under the cloak of the invisible. Breathe through it now. You are never alone. No need to do this on your own. You are safe and supported by non-physical hands. You will know when it is time. Kindness to self is important now.

Chapter 39

~Leaving the Comfort of the Known~

As your heart opens to you, all of you, your forgiveness of both yourself and others in your life opens your heart to a wider, greater experience of love and being love. Those pesky people you once thought were here to make your life hell, or came to make you feel insecure about who you are, become a great gift that life gave you to become the love that you are.

Perhaps a sibling does outstandingly well in every single area you felt lacking in before. They may be younger and be highly confident, succeeding in their chosen career, blissfully happy in their relationships, socially able to converse with all kinds of people, and before, they were a proverbial pain in the butt of your self-worth and self-esteem.

Before you took your journey inward, before you took a step into the 'now' moment, stopped rushing into the future, they were the people who pushed your buttons the most. They were the gate-keepers of your rage, resentment, envy and jealousy. They may even have been the starting block in you comparing yourself negatively with the world around you. Yet now, in the light of a more clear awareness, through forgiving yourself for your judgments of them and you, turning around those judgments of them towards self, you can see you are no different from the judgments you had of them, and from here you are able to see the gift they are.

Life, God, the Divine, gifting you another opportunity to love.

But you had to go through a very dark, and often harsh tunnel, before you saw that it was a gift.

People could have told you years ago that if you just forgave, if you just changed your perception of those in your life, you would be happy, but you could not have heard these people because it was not their job to go through your journey for you. It was yours. And the greatest learning and knowing comes from experience.

A builder does not get up one day and suddenly build himself a house. He needs to learn the tools of the trade, and he needs to know how the structure is formed, what equipment he needs, what type of cement will hold the bricks together, what will keep it warm and how to install windows and doors.

Your journey is no different. You all need to build the foundation of your life through embracing each gift, be it pain, a person, an opportunity or a simple let go. These are the building blocks of your life, and emerging from the cocoon of the known takes place when all the foundations are strong, when the structure is taking shape and eventually you move in.

You own your journey, you move into the real you, the you that has been within you all along. This is your journey, no-one else's. It takes as long as it needs to, in the way it needs to for you to grow and evolve the greatest expression of source energy incarnate in your physical vessel called 'HUMAN'.

Leaving the Comfort of the Known

Emerging from your cocoon is much like a butterfly; you need a little time to dry your wings before you fly. The same goes with moving into a new house. The structure may be there, the rooms are built, the windows and doors are in, but you need to buy some furniture, add the finishing touches, and let go of your old home first.

So from the known to the unknown, it too is a gradual process, and it takes more patience and less haste as this will make the new awakening and opportunities fuller, more vivid and ripe for your new beginning and emergence into the light of who you really are.

Y8 - books not → A3 examples
  - answers on diol

Y7 - Matchsticks
  - xtable sheets
  - ÷ sheets
  - settler

Y9 - Pythag booklet ① x } check!
                    ② x 1 }

  - 'Put in order'
  - Skills check 7-8
           then push 9 to   Momen
                             Rom
                             Torres
                             Aman
                             Dalia
                             Emile